C000213880

It's not every day that you see a great tall old tree fall in j of your very eyes. Not every day that the roots revealed, back, upended, stand higher than your head. The tree bec my adopted tree, and through the year I returned to it now again. I wondered whether the wardens of the park would it away or whether it would be chopped up, wondered whether I could take a little piece of the wood and make something from it – a memoriam. The tree had fallen across a path, and as the year passed, a new path was made through the grass by the feet and the bicycle wheels and the pushchairs of the people who went by. The craggy roots became a climbing frame with earthy foot-holes. You could climb up and see the tree stretched out below you ten or eleven metres down the slope of the hill. It got sprayed on by dogs and with paint; the outermost branches were hacked off; the middle of the trunk became a bouncy hobbyhorse. The tree seemed very noble, very sad, and very dead.

One day, in autumn, when this book was nearly finished, I went to the park to look at my tree again. To my amazement, on the very topmost branch of this horizontal tree, was a tiny spray of bright green leaves. A botanist or horticulturalist, would be able to make some rational sense of this miraculous sprout of life, could say that the specific density and diameter of the trunk, the very make-up of its molecules, enabled it to hold the strength and length of sap required to feed these little shoots. A scientist could explain some deep evolutionary prerogative. A gardener would have a reason. Me? I thought: 'It's a sign!' Although what it meant, I had not a clue.

I have to confess that my first instinct was to pluck that tiny spray of leaves from the tree. I would make it mine: I would take it home and put it in a jar with water and wait for new roots to grow. Who would notice? Who could have watched the tree as assiduously as I had done through the year? By right, I thought, these leaves are mine. But then I wondered whether the leaves, plucked, would survive their transplantation. Would I have to *watch as the final remnant of life in my tree withered and turned brown and died before my eyes at home, fading in a jar of water? Wasn't it better that I let it be?*

    I settled for a photo instead. Here it is.

This is a work about Giulio Camillo,

a Renaissance man who used visual signs to express his message in a short volume called *L'Idea del Theatro*. It was about 'the eternal nature of all things'.[1] Camillo understood that there is an important relationship between the image and memory.

In loving memory of
Harry Stainton & Sibylle Stainton
1909–2005   1922–2005

David Brown
1925–2002

Dedicated with love to my family

A Search for the Source of

The Whirlpool
of Artifice

The Cosmology of Giulio Camillo

Kate Robinson

DUNEDIN ACADEMIC PRESS

EDINBURGH

Published by
Dunedin Academic Press Ltd
Hudson House
8 Albany Street
Edinburgh EH1 3QB
Scotland

ISBN 1 903765 53 6

© 2006 Kate Robinson

The right of Kate Robinson to be identified as the author of this book
has been asserted by her in accordance with sections 77 & 78 of the
Copyright, Designs and Patents Act 1988

All rights reserved.
No part of this publication may be reproduced or transmitted in any form or by
any means or stored in any retrieval system of any nature without prior written
permission, except for fair dealing under the Copyright, Designs and Patents
Act 1988 as amended or in accordance with a licence issued by the Copyright
Licensing Society in respect of photocopying or reprographic reproduction. Full
acknowledgment as to author, publisher and source must be given. Application for
permission for any other use of copyright material should be made in writing to
the publisher.

British Library Cataloguing in Publication Data
A catalogue record for this book is available from the British Library.

Design and pre-press production by Makar Publishing Production, Edinburgh.
Printed and bound in Poland. Produced by Polskabook.

Contents

To see further examples of the
virtual reality model described in
this book, go to www.seedbed.net

A Search for the Source of

The Whirpool of Artifice

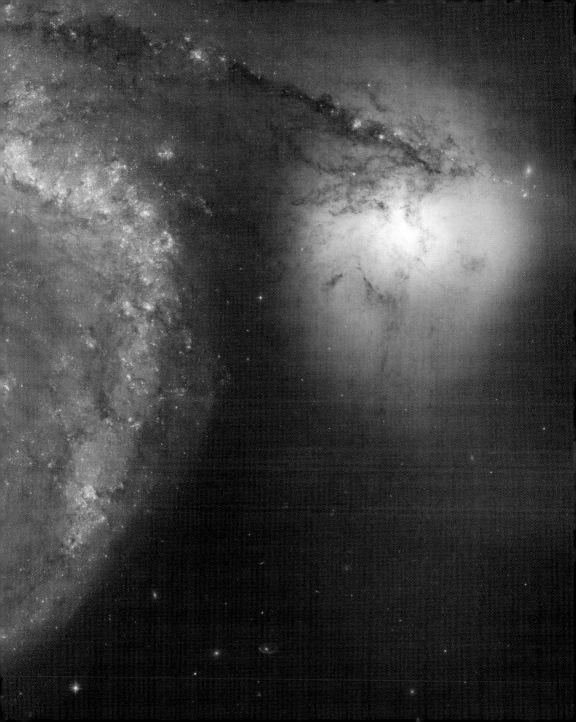

Chapter 1

The Whirlpool

here was a violent storm in January. The wind howled and thin sleet made Glasgow-grey diagonals, and the midday sky was turbulent and wild. Inside, staring at my computer screen, poring over my books, I could hear the windows rattle. Suddenly a walk in the Botanics seemed a much better option than Giulio Camillo.

Created in 1881, the main gates to Glasgow's Botanic Gardens are in the west end, near Byres Road. The Gardens spread out north, and east along the River Kelvin, ending near Charing Cross in the city centre. There are distinct areas of the park that have their own atmosphere, formal and wild. At the Byres Road end are the heated glasshouses where the cyclamen and the palms and the magnolias are kept. Past the University, near the hospital and the municipal art gallery and museum, the park turns into Kelvingrove and has a fountain, and large expanses of green, and a red blaize football pitch. Here is a long formal path between high hedges where in the summer rude red poppies grow and there is a great profusion of flowers that die back again in the autumn. There are sculptures in the gardens. There is a stone lion almost swallowed by rhododendrons and a rampant tiger, carved from wood.

Industry, navigation, commerce and the arts, personified, sit around the bridge near the Art Gallery. Lister and Kelvin sit near the University in a secluded spot. Carlyle stares across the river at a soldier seated on a rock to commemorate the Boer War. At the top of the hill is a sculpture by Harry Bates dedicated to the memory of Field Marshal Earl Roberts, born in India in 1832, who died in France at the beginning of the First World

Lions, Kelvingrove Park

War. His pedestal is flanked with rows of small, turbaned, Indian soldiers, marching into the future. Seated on a horse, high above our heads, Earl Roberts would have a great view of Govan and the river. West of Roberts, in a quiet clearing is a sculpture by Benno Schotz, that looks like a large twig: Psalmist playing on a lyre. Nearby, in Kelvin Way, is an oak tree, planted in April 1918, to commemorate the granting of votes to women. In the centre of the University, close to the Botanics, is a garden opened in 2002, designed by Christine Borland, resulting from her work at the Department of Human Anatomy, where dissections take place. The leaves of flowers and trees are inscribed onto the white, tooth-like, headrests of the benches that are placed here. There is a tiny hole pierced in the centre of each headrest, and a narrow channel cut into the top of each bench. Are these piercings and channels for thoughts, like blood, to flow into the ground? When I was last there, a man lay outstretched on a bench, his head cradled in the October sun.

To return to the walk in the Gardens, in January: there is a little side entrance to the park, near my house, that leads you down to the river through a dishevelled avenue of trees. In the spring it's full of daffodils. In January the tall trunks creaked and the branches sang and thrashed. Despite the storm it wasn't cold. It was exhilarating. There seemed no direction to the wind, it blasted courses from every quarter, pushing great gulps of air into the lungs. Brown leaves hurled around and broken branches lay across the paths. I heard later that slates and chimneys had fallen, roofs blown off, roads blocked. I felt the wind would blow me off my feet. I came to a clearing near the river where the path opens out and there are swings and a slide. Just as I got there, with a sickening click, a tall tree fell. Just like that, with a snap like a twig, it crashed into the green, and almost upon me. 'It's a sign!' I thought. Yes, indeed, the most potent meaning of which, at that point, was to get the hell out of the park. So I ran back home through the wind and the rain to Camillo.

Within an image a pattern of knowledge can be stored, as it can force upon the mind's eye an impression so visceral and emotionally significant that it has the equivalence of a vast data bank. Like a seal in wax, like a signature, images give access to instinctive recall. Camillo describes the universe in highly visual and mythical terms. The world, the planets and history are pictured as a vast network of visual relationships. This imaginary network is arranged within the context of a celestial Theatre. Camillo was funded generously to develop his theories by the King of France, François 1er on one condition: Camillo should not divulge his secret idea to anyone else but the King. Camillo remained true to this stipulation for most of his life: he kept his secret. But then, in Milan, three months before his death in 1544, Camillo told his theories to a trusted friend, Girolamo Muzio. Muzio wrote down everything Camillo said, and *L'Idea del Theatro* was finally published in 1550.

Giulio Camillo, posthumously, was referred to by a number of writers during the seventeenth and eighteenth centuries, including Ariosto and Rousseau; likewise, he was fêted by scientists. A life of Camillo was published in a journal of scientific and philological works in Venice in 1755.[2] Count Federigo Altani details the early years of Camillo and assesses his work in terms of his contribution to science and language. For Altani, the connection between physics and literature was seamless, as it was for the other contributors to this Venetian journal, which was to be published up until 1760.

More recently Camillo's work has been interpreted in terms of a tradition of 'Theatres of Memory'. This tradition has inspired artists from many disparate disciplines: amongst them the writers Philip Pullman (2000) and Carlota Caulfield (2003); visual artists Jean Dubuffet (1977) and Bill Viola (1985) and the composer John Buller (2003).[3] Many of these artists were inspired to write about Camillo because of Frances Yates's influential book, *The Art of Memory* (1966).

For Yates, Camillo's Theatre is the first, in a long Renaissance tradition, of a series of repositories of secret hermetic teachings that reaches its apex in Shakespeare's Globe. Yates brands these secret teachings 'occult Neoplatonism' and identifies:

> the recurrence of a pattern which seems to run through the Renaissance. We saw it first in the Memory Theatre which Giulio Camillo brought as a secret to the King of France. We saw it again in the Memory Seals which [Giordano] Bruno carried from country to country. We see it finally in the Theatre Memory System in the book which [Robert] Fludd dedicated to a King of England. And this system contains, as a secret hidden within it, factual information about the Globe Theatre.[4]

Yates writes about the subject of memory with passion and her book is seductive, sparking off fruitful lines of enquiry. Ted Hughes, in his powerful work *Shakespeare and the Goddess of Complete Being* (1992), talks about the idea of a Memory Theatre as a 'systematically linked hierarchy of images, uniting Heaven and Earth' and goes on to offer a key to a reading

Camillo's Theatre according to Frances Yates.

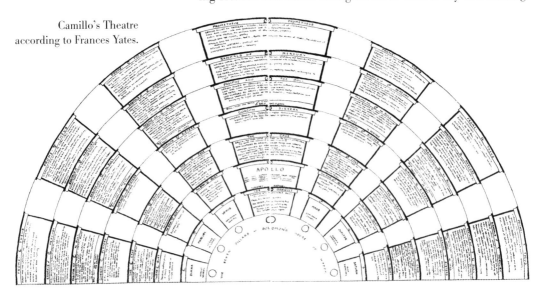

of Shakespeare. This 'basic structural pattern' is a key, which Hughes equates with DNA, operating at the level of the 'poetic organism'.[5]

Based on the assumption that 'Camillo's Memory Theatre [was] . . . a distortion of the plan of the real Vitruvian theatre' Frances Yates created a visual diagram of the images described in *L'Idea del Theatro*. Working with her sister who had studied at Glasgow School of Art, Yates's version of the Theatre is an intriguing section at the centre of *The Art of Memory*. This semicircular arena is filled with tiny, neat handwriting, noting the places where Camillo placed each of the hundreds of images that are described in *L'Idea del Theatro*. It must have taken obsessive patience to complete.

My own introduction to Camillo came via Yates. As a practising sculptor, it resulted in an exhibition.[6] The sculptures in the exhibition were based on mythical motifs represented in Camillo's Theatre, and on current theories based on the function of memory. My response, at this stage, was intuitive. I purposely did not read too much about the man and had not yet seen an original copy of *L'Idea del Theatro*, as I wanted to feel around the subject. It was always my intention, though, after the exhibition was over, to write about Giulio Camillo.

Juno on swing, acrylic on canvas, 2001.

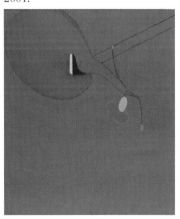

In retrospect, I now see that there was an even division in my exhibition between 'mythical' and 'scientific' approaches to the theme, although, at the time, I was not aware of a conscious decision that this should be so. Of the mythical subjects, sculptures included two suspended figures made of transparent resin, titled *Juno and Apollo*.

The theme of Juno was repeated in a series of paintings: *Juno in the Clouds*. A group of small bronzes, titled *Apollo and the Muses*, showed a male figure surrounded by tall bell-like female forms. *The Furies* was a group of three small female forms cast in cement fondue, with silk shrouds. *Endymion* was a figure cast in white resin, draped in silk.

Other work was based on recent research into the processes of memory. Memory has been called the 'Holy Grail of neuroscience'.[7] From a medical perspective it has been found that it is probably the hippocampus that is responsible for memory. The hippocampus is a tiny sea-horse-shaped organ in the centre of the brain. Inside the hippocampus itself is the amygdala. If the hippocampus is able to store the facts of memories, the amygdala feels them. It is thought that if the amygdala is stimulated – in the sense that it is emotionally aroused – the ability to store information in the hippocampus is increased. In this respect, Giulio Camillo's understanding of the emotive significance of imagery in what we remember was prescient.

Following in a long tradition of artists working in a medical environment, I studied and worked for a period at the Department of Human Anatomy at the University of Glasgow, where I analysed images of the body. In particular, I scrutinized the heart and the brain. I looked at molecular images of the lower, mid and upper pons, for example, and drew what I saw. I used the conventions of the laboratory to make decisions about what sections of the body I would study and I was faithful to what I witnessed

Hippocampus, ink on paper, 2001.

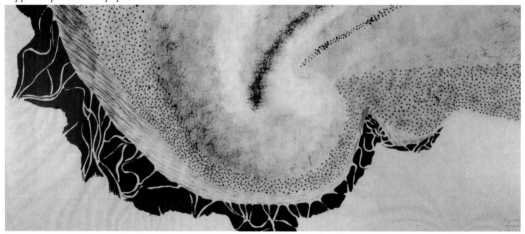

under the microscope. The final piece in the exhibition was a virtual reality model of the Theatre, incorporating computer-generated drawings. Many of the images that are interspersed through this book are from this VRML model, and I shall return to describe it further, in Chapter 7, when I discuss the centre of the Theatre.

Several years have gone by since the exhibition, and now I have studied *L'Idea del Theatro* at first hand, changing my perspective on Camillo's contribution. I received the text around Christmas time. Early one morning, a large package arrived from the USA. It was the unbound facsimile copy of the 1550 edition of *L'Idea del Theatro*, with an English translation and notes by Lu Beery Wenneker.[8] I remember opening the parcel as I lay in bed, the papers spilling all over the covers, snow falling outside, and having the feeling that my relationship with Camillo was still very much alive.

Heart, bronze and stained glass, 2001.

In my first readings of *L'Idea del Theatro*, I was drawn to the Theatre because I felt as though Camillo was telling a story, not in the way that a narrative painting might tell a story, but in the sense that there were connections between each of the images, across the *space* of the Theatre, that he intended the reader/viewer to pluck images from across the entire network of the Theatre and use them to reconstruct, reassemble, a meaningful pattern. Camillo was using a multi-dimensional visual language.

Having read Yates, I was prepared for *L'Idea del Theatro* to be about memory and myths; what surprised me was that instead it appeared to be about the planets. The further I read, the more fascinating it became. It transpired that Camillo was at the centre of a European-wide scandal involving charges of paganism; that his thinking was influenced by radical northern Italian writers such as Francesco Colonna and Pietro d'Abano; and that *L'Idea del Theatro* itself can be read within the context of the astronomy of the time. Camillo was turning, in front of my eyes, from being a myth-maker to a star-gazer.

Camillo was certainly not without his detractors. Even his earliest promoter was equivocal: Lodovico Domenichi, in his dedicatory letter to Don Diego Hurtado,[9] of the first edition of *L'Idea del Theatro* implied that Camillo's reputation may have suffered because he had 'promised too much'.[10] Tiraboschi, writing in 1824, said that the Theatre was a 'vain and incredible thing'.[11] The Scottish Reverend J.A. Wylie, in his massive three-volume history of Protestantism published in 1878 dismissed this 'dark-visaged man . . . around whom there seemed ever to hover an air of mystery' as an intellectual butterfly.[12] Within the last fifty years, he has variously been called 'one of the most famous men of the sixteenth century',[13] the 'peak of absurdity',[14] 'an amusing . . . imposter',[15] and recently the 'great actor of the Renaissance'.[16] Yates, herself, was ambiguous: while two whole chapters of *The Art of Memory* were devoted to Camillo and the Theatre, he is made out to be a bit of a buffoon, a stammerer, 'Poor Camillo'.[17]

Perhaps Camillo provoked such a mixed response because *L'Idea del Theatro* is such an unusual book. Essentially about the planets and the layout of the heavens, it also touches on medicine, myth, philosophy, theology and social commentary. The broadness of Camillo's scope, in itself, was not necessarily unique. Other writers of the period such as Giovanni Pontano and Sacro Bosco were wide-ranging in the themes they treated. What marks out Camillo is his reliance on the visual image – the sign – to reveal his meaning. *L'Idea del Theatro* contains over two hundred distinct visual metaphors, which are graphically described in text, although there are no drawings, as such. An illustrated copy of *L'Idea del Theatro* by Titian, with whom Camillo was acquainted, did not survive a fire at El Escorial in 1671. A great pity, as it must have been a magnificent object to behold.

In the British Library a copy of Petrarch's poems, printed by Aldus Manutius (Aldo Manuzio) in 1514, includes the hand-written notes of Giulio Camillo. In tiny, precise letters in red and sepia ink, his words mark the margins as well as blank pages inserted into the printed script. The precision and detail of his notes are alluring. On page forty-nine of this copy of the *Canzoniere*, Camillo has inserted a tiny watercolour drawing at the bottom of the page. It shows a landscape with trees and rolling hills and a small town in the distance with a spire and a dome. It's quite crudely painted, and the colours are dull, but it lights up the text. I think that this image may be inserted here because, for Camillo, the number forty-nine was important and he wanted to highlight the significance of the page number. The forty-nine words of the Lord's Prayer made it an auspicious, or magical, number.[18] The number seven – or seven times seven – was later to become for Camillo similarly important in the arrangement of the Theatre.

For a number of reasons, I was able to spend only a few minutes with this book in the Library. I didn't attempt to analyse the text in detail. I tried purely to get an impression of Camillo from the marks he made, rather than the sense of what he said. And I admit that his script surprised me. Camillo's prose, captured by Muzio in *L'Idea del Theatro*, is flamboyant, if not flowery. He digresses in wild tangents, spiralling into endless sentences made of impossible clauses. Sometimes it's difficult to keep the thread. And yet his handwriting, here on the pages of the *Canzoniere*, was measured and economical. It was balanced, methodical, precise. He clearly had an eye for the layout of a page, knowing how and where to place his words in order to contain the maximum amount of information.

To play, for a moment, Devil's advocate, I had to ask whether these annotations by Camillo were the mark of a man who could be charged with being, as Erasmus accused him, a 'Nosoponus'. There seems to be something random and illogical, even capricious, in imposing on Petrarch an interpretation that is so arbitrary as to depend on page number. Captivating as his script appeared, was its insertion nevertheless without meaning? Of course my answer to this devilish, doubting question is: No. The ink from Camillo's quill expresses precisely his dedication to, and openness about, his own idiosyncratic response to phenomena. It is from his subjectivity that I think Camillo has so much to offer. His peculiarity marks him out. Camillo resolutely witnesses the world from his own point of view, which leads him to describe a robust and vital philosophy. But I have borne the doubt and carried the question, instigated by Erasmus, Tiraboschi, Bolgar and others, throughout my enquiry, at the forefront of my mind. It added spice.

This book about Camillo has grown out of a desire to understand the currents of thought that formed him. *L'Idea del Theatro* was composed when printing was in its infancy; in fact, it wasn't necessarily meant to be printed at all. So it offers an unadulterated glimpse of the mental map of an early sixteenth century man, opening a doorway to a lost world where the boundaries between medicine, art and the stars were very different from what they are now. I see the book as a natural progression from my sculptural research and, in a sense, I have adopted Camillo's methods as my own. Camillo explored space using images and words, and so have I.

Chapter 2 begins with a brief biography of Camillo, and then there is a description of the Theatre. The emphasis is on an interpretation of the upper levels of the Theatre from the 'Banquet' to 'Prometheus'. These are the levels concerned with nature, art and man. I will look at Frances Yates's version of the Theatre as well as other models of 'data space' suggested by the artist Bill Viola. I hope that this will give a flavour of *L'Idea del Theatro* as a whole.

Chapter 3 focuses on Erasmus, the great humanist philologist and translator, at the heart of whose *Ciceronianus* (1528) Camillo is mentioned. Erasmus and Camillo met in Italy, either in Venice or Rome. I ask why it was that Erasmus was so threatened by Camillo, and suggest that Erasmus – a western icon of

rational humanist thought – has 'magical' roots to his thinking. At any rate, Camillo's theories and discoveries discomfited
Erasmus, though they equally enthralled him, bringing down
a rain of vitriol in *Ciceronianus* that was to send shock waves
through Europe.

Chapters 4 and 5 are based on a comparison between the
work of Francesco Colonna and Camillo. Colonna is an intriguing and shadowy character. His *Hypnerotomachia Poliphili* was
published anonymously by Aldus Manutius in 1499. It was years
later that the identity of the author was revealed, and even now
it is still contested. Variously described, Colonna may have been
a Venetian monk or a Roman prince. His work has famously
defied categorization, being described as an erotic novella,
a handbook of alchemy, or even as a garden-design manual.
Whatever Colonna's origin, there are a number of striking correlations between his work and that of Camillo. Even though
the form of the two books is widely divergent, they both rely on
signs and share central motifs.

Chapter 4 looks at issues regarding each author's use of
emblematic material, and addresses their work in terms of
memory practice and the uses of hieroglyphic and iconographic
grammar. I will look in detail at two of their shared emblematic
motifs and examine how these may be interpreted in terms of
theories of 'mythical time'. I will examine how each author uses
a technique of progressive interpretation of an image in order to
present his message. I also look at the Aristotelian doctrine of
the *topics*, and how this was to affect their work.

Chapter 5 assesses Colonna's influence on Camillo in terms
of the motif of a Theatre to describe planetary arrangement. It
discusses the possible influence that Camillo and Colonna were
to make on the 'theatres' at, for example, the *Orto Botanico*
– the first Botanic Gardens created at Padua in 1545 – and the
first anatomy theatre, also at Padua, created around 1582. This
chapter will also begin to unravel some of the scientific theories

with which Camillo was involved, which, like Colonna's, were based on the assumption of the cosmic influence of divine love in a world in which all that is visible, as well as aspects that they believed were hidden, is holy.

The penultimate chapter assesses Camillo's *L'Idea del Theatro* in terms of its place in the history of astronomy. A critique of contemporary astronomy written in 1581 by the Jesuit professor, Christopher Clavius, details a number of heterodox cosmologies in evidence in Italy which all provided new accounts of the universe at odds with the prevailing Ptolemaic orthodoxy. Direct comparisons can be made between aspects of these heterodox theories and *L'Idea del Theatro*, particularly the 'celestial channels' theory. The final part of the chapter will make a literary comparison between *L'Idea del Theatro* and Copernicus's *De Revolutionibus*, and discuss Camillo's theories regarding planetary arrangement and the movement of the earth.

The final chapter assesses the innermost part of the Theatre. While Camillo describes physical space, he also talks about philosophical space, and our relationship to it. I discuss the idea of the 'vanishing point' and perspectival theory, in relation to the images of the Theatre, and end by asking whether there is a single unifying position within the Theatre that is able to reconcile its 'diverse imaginations'. An Epitaph for Camillo is based on an interpretation of an emblem made in his memory by Achille Bocchi, first printed in 1555.

Before turning to Chapter 2, I would like to mention a motif in Camillo's *Trattato delle materie*. In this, he describes an *artificiosa rota*, or artificial wheel. The *artificiosa rota* fits within a long tradition of mnemonic, rhetorical and scientific wheels dating from the twelfth century in evidence throughout Europe.[19] The purpose of Camillo's wheel was literary: it was designed to enable Camillo to compose a sonnet in celebration of a Duke.[20] The wheel is interesting because it shows how

Camillo played with text. In this spiralling circular arrangement Camillo fools around with ideas, with words and even emotions. He calls the centre, or 'generative nucleus', of the wheel the 'whirlpool of artifice'.[21]

Camillo's philosophy and working method was based on the conviction that the sum total of all things – all material, every topic – as well as every word, was reducible to a number of finite elements. The *artificiosa rota* worked on the idea of uniting literary opposites. Material, or topics – ideas in literary form – were placed at each position on the spokes of the wheel, arranged in such a way that the reverse, or opposite, of a topic was placed on each opposing spoke, for example, 'arrival' and 'departure'.

Camillo thought that through playing with a text, deconstructing it, reassembling it, teasing and coaxing it into extremes, new patterns of language could evolve out of the old. What he called the 'golden age' of language could provide the raw materials for a revival of the new. It was *serio ludere*, or serious play. An outcome of the continuing fascination with the production of perfect rhetoric and literary style the games diced with artifice in the name of authenticity. They were the games that were to infuriate Erasmus and draw his vitriol in *Ciceronianus*.

According to Camillo, it was inside the whirlpool of artifice, at the centre of the imaginary wheel, that his rhetorical game was played. His simile of a whirlpool was not accidental. In the centre of the whirlpool there was space for the hidden and uncontrollable, a space for language, for the sign, to disintegrate and re-form. He thought that here opposites could be reconciled, material changed, transmutation made possible. All of Camillo's work was dedicated to the search for the *locus* of transformation. All signs, whether man-made or divine, were the material for this conversion. Art, as well as God's Book of Nature, were fair game. The *artificiosa rota* was a literary conversion; Camillo's *L'Idea del Theatro*, meanwhile, was astronomical.

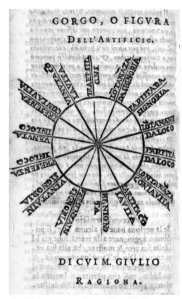

Artificiosa rota, from Camillo's 'Opere' (Venice: Farri, 1579).

Chapter **2**   Camillo

e was born in Friuli, in the north-east of Italy, in around 1480. Sandwiched, from north to south, between the Alps and the Adriatic and flanked from east to west, by Slovenia, and the Veneto, the region had been an important strategic centre since Roman times. From the sixth century it had been home to the Christian Patriarch of Aquileia, in constant conflict with Rome. In the early fifteenth century, after its defeat by the powerful Republic of Venice, it was famous for its mercury mines, its witches and its alchemy. Around the time of Camillo's birth it was in the throes of one of the earliest of the peasant revolts that were to ripple throughout the Continent.

Biographical details of the early life of Camillo are sparse, and his biographers contradictory. His childhood was probably spent in Portogruaro. He took his family name, Delminio, from the birthplace of his father, in Dalmatia, in what is now Croatia. He studied philosophy and jurisprudence at the University of Padua in the years around 1500, and subsequently taught eloquence and logic at San Vito, an academy in Friuli. In 1508, he was involved in the short-lived Accademia Liviana at Pordenone. The Academy was founded by the Venetian General Bartholomeo d'Alviano in a temporary respite from battles in Padua instigated by the League of Cambrai and attracted an eclectic mix of brilliant and radical thinkers. Here, Camillo would have come in contact with the astronomer and physician, Girolamo Fracastoro, and the poets, Giovanni Cotta and Antonio Navagero. The painter, Raphael – though not at the Academy – was to paint a portrait of Navagero, which hangs now in Rome.[1] Girolamo Fracastoro created one of the first orrerys – a working model of the cosmos – though he believed that the earth rather than the sun was at the centre.

Around the first decade of the sixteenth century, Camillo lived in Venice where he was in close contact with some of the most influential writers and artists of Europe. He stayed near the house of the famous printer, Aldus Manutius, in the Sestiere di San Polo, in the centre of the city. He knew the Dutch philologist Desiderius Erasmus and worked with the painter, Titian (Tiziano Vecellio). He was part of the cultural circle that included Aretin and Bembo and had personal ties with the architect, Serlio, and his family.[2] During this time, Camillo spent considerable care in charting regional differentiations in the Friulian dialect and was a champion of the local use of Italian, rather than Latin. And of course he was working on his ideas for the theatre.[3]

Camillo is believed to have held a chair of Dialectics at the University of Bologna from around 1521 to 1525, and is known to have been at the Coronation of Charles V in 1529. The following year, when Camillo was around fifity years old, he journeyed to Paris at the invitation of King François 1er. Two others – Count Rangone and Camillo's agent, Girolamo Muzio – accompanied him on the long journey from the Veneto. Camillo appears to have been a man of some physical presence and to have made an impression in Paris. There is a story that one day, 'in a room with many gentlemen at some windows looking out over a garden,' he was confronted with a lion that had escaped from its cage. 'Drawing near to him from behind, with its paws, [the lion] took [Camillo] without harm by the thighs, and with its tongue, proceeded to lick him.' ' . . . That touch and . . . that breath, himself being overturned . . . all the others having fled'[4] appears to have had a profound effect on Camillo, and images of lions appear often in his writings. The lion story was corroborated by a number of sources and cannot have harmed Camillo's mystique.[5]

He made his name as an orator and wrote on principles of eloquence, which circulated Paris in manuscript, though these works were not published until later. *Trattato dell' Imitazione*,[6] his reponse to criticisms made by Erasmus, for example, was written in Paris. Camillo produced a manuscript titled *Theatro della Sapientia*, in 1530, for François, in which his ideas for the Theatre were outlined. He impressed François with his proposals and was given funds by the King to develop his ideas.

Camillo was back in Italy by the end of 1531, and stayed in Venice and Bologna. He then returned to France in 1533 and appears to have kept the French connection going till around 1537. Throughout this period, he was working on the Theatre. Eventually, though, remuneration from the King began to dry up and Camillo decided to return to Italy for good. During the latter part of 1543, or very early in 1544, he accepted an offer brokered by Girolamo Muzio to go to Milan. Here, in Milan, at the court of the Marchese del Vasto, after much persuasion, Camillo finally dictated his great idea to Muzio who transcribed all he said, over the course of seven days and nights; an apocryphal tale has it that they both lounged on adjoining beds while Camillo held forth, in emulation of the ancient philosophers. The manuscript was completed early in February 1544. Three months later, on 15 May, Camillo died.

Strangely, Muzio and the Marchese del Vasto decided not to publish Camillo's thesis, even though they had gone to such lengths to acquire it. Camillo's idea languished. It was not until six years later that it was to receive a wider public, when the manuscript turned up in the hands of Antonio Cheluzzi da Colle. Da Colle put the text in order, and *L'Idea del Theatro* was finally published in 1550, in Florence, by Lorenzo Torrentino.

L'Idea del Theatro

So, what was in *L'Idea del Theatro?* What did it contain to convince Muzio and del Vasto to put off publication? The book is arranged in seven sections that chart the creation of the world. Camillo speaks of a system that, as he says, makes 'scholars into spectators'. He is imagining a theatre in its original sense – as a place in which a spectacle unfolds:

> **Following the order of the creation of the world, we shall place on the first levels the more natural things . . . those we can imagine to have been created before all other things by divine decree. Then we shall arrange from level to level those that followed after, in such a way that in the seventh, that is, the last and highest level shall sit all the arts . . . not by reason of unworthiness, but by reason of chronology, since these were the last to have been found by men.**[7]

Camillo believed the world was made of 'primary matter'. This primary matter was sometimes called 'hyle'; it is the material of all that is manifest.[8] Camillo thought that by reducing knowledge into its constituent parts, you could come closer to comprehending hyle, the original essence, and consequently understand what makes the world tick. Likewise (but in reverse), through comprehending the universe you would understand its essential ingredients. His key to this was in the creation of a symbolic system that both represented the essence of material, as well as the relationships between the essences that allowed the universe to maintain its being. The 'idea of the Theatre' was fundamentally a structure of conceptual relationships rather than a building of wood or stone, and it is on that level that Camillo's work bears most fruit. The Theatre is to be understood in terms of time and space – a spatial representation of chronology.

The entire Theatre, says Camillo, rests on Solomon's Seven Pillars of Wisdom, outwith which number 'nothing else can be imagined'. On the Seven Pillars rest the planets, which govern, or administrate, 'cause and effect'. Camillo names these planets: the Moon, Mercury, Venus, Mars, Jupiter and Saturn. He omits the name of the Earth. Arranged in an ascending order from the planets, and affected by their influence, are a further six levels, which, broadly speaking, represent a gradual development from nature to art. These upper levels are named: the Banquet, the Cave, the Gorgons, Pasiphae, the Sandals of Mercury, and Prometheus. The Banquet and the Cave are the most 'elemental' of the levels where creation first began. The levels of the Gorgons, and Pasiphae, are where the 'inner' man is revealed in relation to the cosmos; these levels are part nature, part art. The levels of the Sandals of Mercury and Prometheus are concerned specifically with man as an active agent within the world, or art and man. I will go into more detail about the upper levels later in this chapter and discuss the innermost level of the Theatre, where the planets are located, in Chapters 6 and 7.

The Grid

The naming of the levels in effect creates a grid system. Within this system are placed the images. It is a grid system to enhance memory, and also to affect the interpretation of a given image. Rather than a graph based on numeric values, the values in Camillo's scheme are based on language and myth. I discuss the use of this grid of meaning further in Chapter 4, and look at the ways in which Camillo assumed the progressive interpretation of an image at different positions within the Theatre. Using progressive interpretation, Camillo is able to use several images again and again, their meaning subtly altered by their position within the Theatre. Camillo describes around two hundred images all of which are evocative and multi-layered. In Chapter 4 I analyse two of them: the 'Elephant' and the 'Wolf, Lion and Dog'.

According to the life written by Altani, Camillo had studied at the 'humanist cathedral' of Lazaro Bonamico,[9] and, though not explicitly acknowledged by Camillo, *L'Idea del Theatro* owes much to the writings of Marsilio Ficino, Pico della Mirandola and Lorenzo Valla.[10] In common with other philosophical/scientific authors of the period, Camillo backs up his theories by referring to biblical and classical sources,[11] notably Lucretius's *De Rerum Natura*.[12] The whole work is liberally peppered with references to cabbalistic writings; Camillo, living in cosmopolitan Venice, clearly enjoyed intellectual commerce with his Jewish neighbours.[13] The highly complex system of the cabbalah involves the analysis of the 'Sfirot', or divine powers. There are a number of visual representations of this, all involving the theoretical arrangement of the Sfirot in spatial relationships, which tend to branch out in tree-like formations. There is evidence, however, that the cabbalah was not a subject that was wholly to absorb Camillo, and that he later felt that the references to it in *L'Idea del Theatro* were more like spice than the meat of the work.[14]

An example of a Sfirot Tree.[15]

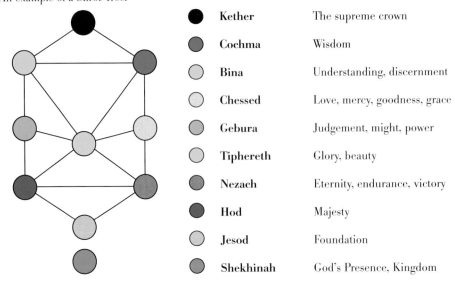

⬤	**Kether**	The supreme crown
⬤	**Cochma**	Wisdom
⬤	**Bina**	Understanding, discernment
⬤	**Chessed**	Love, mercy, goodness, grace
⬤	**Gebura**	Judgement, might, power
⬤	**Tiphereth**	Glory, beauty
⬤	**Nezach**	Eternity, endurance, victory
⬤	**Hod**	Majesty
⬤	**Jesod**	Foundation
⬤	**Shekhinah**	God's Presence, Kingdom

The Body

Scattered throughout *L'Idea del Theatro* are references to the body, explaining Camillo's theory that the 'inner' and the 'outer' man correspond to each other through a system of vital equivalence. Medieval medicinal practices routinely connected the assumed attributes of particular planets to areas of the body, for example, the feet were associated with Jupiter, the head and genitals with Mars. Camillo makes some moderate changes to this scheme. He suggests that while the head is associated with warlike Mars, the hair, beard, all the skin of the body and also the brain, due to their qualities of 'attraction' and 'dampness', should be consigned to the moon. This anticipates Camillo's discussion of the action of 'celestial streams', connecting the supercelestial and celestial regions in which the hair, beard and skin are the human conduits of heavenly power.

At the Venus/Cave combination, there is the image, among other things, of a three-headed Cerberus. Camillo explains that the animal is three-headed 'to symbolize the three natural necessities, which are eating, drinking and sleeping'. He says that these necessities 'hinder man from his meditation' and describes the story of Aeneas who, 'wishing to pass to the contemplation of lofty things', threw to Cerberus a mouthful of food; Camillo interprets the story to mean that 'if we wish to have time to contemplate' we must satisfy our three bodily necessities 'with little'.[16] However the images of the bodily necessities are given to Venus because of the 'pleasure' associated with them. The same image on the level of Prometheus stands for cooking delicious feasts and the delights suitable to sleep. Scents and cleanliness are to be found at the level of Venus, as well as natural and desirable beauty, represented by Narcissus.

Camillo talks about feet relating to the emotions. Different parts of the foot relate to subtly different emotional states. Under the Gorgons of Venus, for example, an image of Eurydice bitten

Eurydice at the level of the Gorgons.
Emotions governed by our will.

on the heel by a serpent, 'signifies our emotions governed by our will'. Under the Gorgons of Mars, the figure of a young girl with a bare foot indicates 'a decision, or a purpose which is rigid and born suddenly'. He mentions the myth of Achilles, who having been immersed in the Stygian waters, 'became invulnerable in all parts except in the feet,' which he interprets as meaning that he was 'able to be faithful in all parts provided that he was not touched in his emotions'. Camillo equates the washing of the Disciples' feet by Christ, as a washing of their emotions:

> He . . . washed the feet at his departure, that is, the emotions of his Apostles.[17]

False Idols

Although Camillo is not a politically minded man, he is openly critical, in *L'Idea del Theatro*, of aspects of the clergy and the army, censuring both for their idolatry of ambition. He says that this relates to 'two most serious sins'. One is of not worshipping God 'truly and only'. The other is even worse, and this is of adoring the gods 'which we ourselves make within us'. In true Camillan fashion, he turns on its head the usual objections to priestly incontinence, in favour of chastising them for chastity. He says:

> . . . many of those hallowed heads in monasteries have made within themselves an idol of their continence and chastity . . . and so they have raised within their imagination a Vestal goddess.[18]

The army, likewise, comes in for severe words:

> The princes of the army have raised in their heart the deity of Mars. Nor do they only esteem and worship it, but they would like all to bow to it.

But he is unspecific about which particular princes it is with whom he takes issue with. It is unusual of him to make such a specific political comment – he usually steers clear of temporal matters, and he quickly qualifies his statement by generalizing on the moral nature of ambition. 'To speak briefly, ' he says, 'we all have within, a bold and proud lion, which symbolizes our wicked and untamed ambition . . . it is the new god which we have within us.' If we wish to have a spirit strong as Hercules, we must 'kill this lion'. Humility, he says, will follow.

The Vernacular

Before moving on to take a closer look at each of the levels in the Theatre there is one other general point to be made about *L'Idea del Theatro:* it is written in Italian, rather than Latin. The question of the use of Latin versus the vernacular was a thorny issue at this time, an argument in which Camillo was himself actively involved. He was an advocate of Latin, esteeming it as a 'golden' language, but, equally, he was a strong promoter of the use of Italian. It may have been because it was initially dictated rather than written down, that *L'Idea del Theatro* was in the vernacular. Though equally it may have been a careful decision of Camillo to compose the work in Italian, following his heroes, Dante and Petrarch. Petrarch had been instrumental in invigo-rating Italian as a literary language, while Dante begins his cos-mological treatise, *The Banquet*, with a complex argument about why that work is written in the vernacular. In *L'Idea del Theatro* Camillo explicitly refers to aspects of Dante's work, naming one whole level of the Theatre, the Banquet, and it seems probable that he is following his champion in using Italian.[19]

The Levels of the Theatre

The Banquet

The Banquet is where the essential productions of God originate. There are two essential productions, 'one from within the essence of His divinity, and the other from without'. The production from

Proteus, at the level of the Banquet. *Proteus of many shapes . . . signifies primary matter . . . wherein shall be discussed . . . Chaos.*

within is 'consubstantial . . . coessential and eternal': this is the Word of God. The production from without is made 'of nothing . . . in time'. This is primary matter, 'otherwise called Chaos, and by the Platonists, the world soul, and by the poets, Proteus.'[20]

Camillo gives the analogy of 'a mass of unworked wool', from which a cap, a cloak and hose might be formed, to suggest the initial amorphous nature of primary matter. At the level of the Banquet, the 'elements' are most 'simple'; they have not yet been 'mixed'. Camillo says that it is the Spirit of Christ that is responsible for the union of the elements into new forms. Without the Spirit of Christ 'opposites would never be in harmony', and the 'hidden seed of plants and flowers' would not 'unfold'.[21]

He discusses the 'Gamone' of the Pythagoreans, a system based on light, heat and generation, providing the single thing in the book that comes close to a diagram:

He explains that the nature of primary matter is 'watery'.[22] He says that the eternity of the species is established in the Banquet:

> . . . species remain eternal, while the individuals are transitory and mortal. Therefore, although the individuals transform themselves and deteriorate or conceal themselves, nevertheless the species and the eternal Ideas live on . . .[23]

Sun	Light God, the Creator	Flame Word, the example	Brilliance Hyle, Primary Matter	Heat	Generation

The Gamone

The 'Ideas' are the 'forms and exemplars of essential things in the eternal mind . . . whence all things created drew their being'. They bear 'as from seals', the impression of God. The heavens and the earth are 'continually under the wheel . . . of manifestation . . . and concealment'. Birth and death are illusions; there is only consciousness and oblivion.

The Cave

If the Banquet was like the primal soup, then the Cave is more like a hearty stew. The Cave is the third level of the Theatre, in which 'according to the nature of its planet . . . [are kept] the compounds and elements pertaining to it'.[24] Again Camillo talks at length about the power of the Spirit of Christ reconciling opposites, and allowing the earth to be fruitful. In this level the elements have become mixed; it is where matter and form evolve from the exalted Ideas of the Banquet.

The Cave separates the supercelestial from the celestial, so that the influx of the 'supercelestial streams' does not 'rain more than might be suitable for the capacity of matter'.[25] Camillo distinguishes between a Platonic and Homeric Cave, saying that the Theatre's Cave is specifically Homeric. The Platonic Cave is where protagonists watch the projection of images of the world rather than witnessing the real thing. The Homeric Cave, according to Camillo, is where transformation takes place – the transformation of 'weavings and manufacturings' like bees making honey and nymphs weaving cloth.

Atoms at the level of the Cave.
Atoms shall indicate . . . discriminate quantity.

The Gorgons

In the myth, the three sisters named the Gorgons were Medusa, Stheno and Euryale. Serpent-haired, the sisters lived in an inaccessible crag, and had the power of turning their enemies into stone, just by looking at them. The hero, Perseus, assisted by magical sandals that enabled him to fly, a helmet that made him invisible, and a mirror, managed to decapitate Medusa, and threw her head into a bag. From the stump of Medusa's neck sprang Pegasus, the flying horse, and Chrysasor, a warrior with a golden sword. The head of Medusa became the boss on Athena's shield.

The level of the Gorgons is the first to relate to man. Specifically it relates to the 'inner man'. Camillo says that 'it should be

A girl at the level of the Gorgons.
. . . a young girl ascending through Capricorn shall indicate . . . the ascent of the soul into Heaven.

indicated that most of [the] times when the Scriptures mention man, they mean only inner man'.[26] The external man is clothed with skin and flesh, bones and sinews, while the inner man is the image of the divine. The inner man was made by God at an early stage, before the earthly body, in the supercelestial region. He was formed from the 'slime' of the earth. This is not a pejorative term, says Camillo, but signifies 'the flower, and . . . cream of the earth, which was virginal'. This virginal earth is equated with the name of 'Adema, whence Adam drew his name'.[27] Speaking of Adam before he sinned, Camillo goes on to talk about the 'garden of delights'. He says that Adam was 'in the supercelestial garden, not in person, but in the grace of God, rejoicing in all the blessed influences'.

Following the cabbalists, Camillo says that man has three souls: the Nephes, the Ruach and the Nessamah. The Nephes is like a 'shadow', and can be tempted by demons; the Nessamah is closer to the angels and God; 'The poor creature in the middle is goaded by both parts'.[28] The 'inner man' also has three intellects: 'intelligence', which is innate; 'practical intellect', which can be learned; and the 'active intellect', which is the 'power through which we understand'. The 'active intellect' or divine ray is outside us, and under the authority of God'.[29] He has chosen the symbol of the Gorgons because according to the myth, the sisters 'only had one eye between them which was commutable, since the one was able to lend it to another . . .'.[30] This relates to the three souls and the three intellects of man, and 'causes us to understand the divine ray to be without and not within ourselves'.

Pasiphae

The myth of Pasiphae and the bull pertains 'not only to the inner man, but . . . also . . . the exterior'. The father of Pasiphae was Helios, the Sun. Pasiphae married Minos, the King of Crete.

Minos had promised to sacrifice a white bull that appeared from the sea, sent by Poseidon. But when Minos saw the beauty of the bull, he substituted another in its place, and kept the white bull from the sea, in his palace. In revenge at Minos's trickery, Poseidon caused Pasiphae to lust after the magical bull and she forced Daedalus to make the hollow body of an artificial cow, in which she hid herself, to enrapture it. The Minotaur was born from their union, subsequently hidden away in the depths of the labyrinth.

Pasiphae and the Bull.
Pasiphae . . . in love with the bull . . . signifies the soul which . . . falls into covetousness of the body.

According to Camillo, Pasiphae 'signifies the soul . . . [falling] into covetousness of the body.' Quoting from the Psalms, 'Who maketh thy angels spirits, and thy ministers a burning fire',[31] he equates the supercelestial world with fire, while the world below is airy. The simulated cow designed by Daedalus 'stands for the simulated airy body.' The union of a 'thing so pure' (soul) with 'a thing so gross' (body) is made possible by this imitation-mediator. He equates the myth with Platonic philosophy, and describes how in the upper regions, in the supercelestial world, the soul needs a 'fiery vehicle' in which to move its ethereal body, 'because one does not move a thing unless by means of a body'. As the soul descends to the lower regions, and is 'provided with the earthly vehicle in the maternal womb', it changes from fire to air. He says that when 'sinful souls' are 'freed from the earthly vehicle' they are not freed from the air. Therefore they must go to a place of 'cleansing, where they reside until they are free from the airy vehicle and are returned to pure fire, in which they ascend to the holy place.'[32]

The Sandals of Mercury

Mercury was cunning, eloquent and persuasive. In return for becoming the messenger of the Gods, Mercury promised never again to tell a lie, though he said he could not promise always to tell the whole truth. His winged sandals enable him to move

The Winged Sandals of Mercury.
The operations which man can perform
naturally and without any art . . .

as quickly as air. He was patron of travellers and of comerce; he was a cattle-thief and the protector of shepherds; he invented the lyre.

The level of the Sandals of Mercury represents 'all of the operations . . . which man can perform naturally and without any art'. This includes, for example, images to represent 'the midwife who delivers children and the office of washing them'; 'giving or receiving business'; 'supplying, investigating . . . industry'; 'purging and cleansing'; 'making beautiful'; 'enjoying oneself, rejoicing, laughing, making laugh, comforting, making merry'; 'giving oneself airs'; 'dissimulation, cunning or deceit'; 'vigour or strength, or in truth to work towards the truth'.

Prometheus

The seventh and final level is 'assigned to all the arts, noble as well as vile'.[33] Camillo quotes the story of Prometheus and Epimetheus and their distribution of gifts to the animals, from Plato's *Protagorus*.[34] Epimetheus distributed gifts to all the animals, but forgot about man. Prometheus secretly stole, with fire, the knowledge of skill in the arts. However, political wisdom was still in the keeping of Jupiter, who, finally moved to pity by human unhappiness, sent Mercury who was to take to men respect for others and a sense of justice. Camillo says that for this reason, this level not only represents the arts 'but also political and martial powers'.

In this level, Camillo includes military arts and war on land and sea, as well as martial games, arrest, imprisonment, torture and torments. Likewise he includes 'skills done by benefit of the air, such as windmills'. Conversion, consent, sanctity, humility and religion all come under this level, and so do 'the blacksmith's craft of fire', 'the arts of the horse', the slaughterhouse and the criminal and civil courts. Camillo also includes astrology, geometry, geography, cosmography, agriculture and grammar,

Vulcan at the level of Prometheus.
Vulcan shall give us the blacksmith's
craft of fire.

as well as 'the arts pertaining to leather and skins', snaring with night birds and all those condemned to the mill.

The Arrangement

On reading *L'Idea del Theatro*, it is not easy to imagine what arrangement Camillo had in mind. Although he is clear that there are seven levels to the Theatre, his references to exactly *where* specific images are to be inserted, at least on a cursory inspection, seem quite chaotic. Frances Yates's version of the layout, illustrated in Chapter 1, was based on a Vitruvian grid. But in fact Camillo's Theatre is not as ordered and evenly proportioned as a Vitruvian theatre.[35] This unevenness is missing in Yates's picture of the Theatre.

It can be helpful, here, to look at mnemonic trees, used at the Accademia Veneziana. Founded in 1557, and dedicated to the encyclopaedic organization and publication of knowledge, the Academy's editorial programme had been greatly influenced by Camillo, amongst others.[36] Mnemonic trees, as illustrated on the right, were advocated by the Academy as a visual means of the organization of data. Rhetorical in origin, the trees were a method of systematizing words and ideas, of making *material* visually memorable and diagrammatic.

Rhetorical tree diagram, by Giulio Camillo. *Opere* (Venice: Farri, 1579).

A mnemonic tree will begin with certain basic premises or ideas, which are then developed in branching structures. From a visual perspective, the trees are organic, rather than uniform, in shape. Some ideas will, literally, be more fruitful than others, leading to a greater yield of further concepts.

The lists of images in Camillo's *L'Idea del Theatro* reads, in many ways, like a mnemonic tree. An important 'stem' image, for example, a planet, will lead to further images that branch from it. The branching images are no less important, or significant, than the stem image, but they have less structural power within the general scheme. The stem images, like the basic principles within a mnemonic tree are the tenets on which the rest of the imagery and ideas are fundamentally based. I shall discuss this phenomenon further in Chapter 4, and look at the way that Camillo uses an image, with this technique, to develop a theme. But though the mnemonic tree structure is important in understanding the shape of the Theatre, it still does not give the full picture.

Bill Viola's 1995 essay 'Will There Be Condominiums in Data Space?', in which he mentions Camillo, discusses the visual representation of 'data structures'. Viola shows three diagrams that exemplify different approaches to the organization and visualization of a collection of data. The first is a 'branching structure'. Borrowed from the terminology of computer science, and used in interactive games, Viola says that in a branching structure the viewer 'proceeds from top to bottom in time'. He gives the analogy of an interactive virtual tour of the desert, in which the viewer can stop to examine all of the various flora and fauna of the valley floor. But despite this system's interactivity, basically it is 'still the same old linear logic system in a new bottle'.[37]

Tongue in cheek, Viola offers new models for structuring data. He calls one a Matrix Structure. This is a 'non-linear array of information', in which the viewer/protagonist can enter at any point and move in any direction. In this structure, 'All directions are equal.' This, he says, would be an 'area of intelligent perception and thought structures, albeit artificial.' The Matrix should not be understood as a two-dimensional square grid on a flat surface, but a three- or four-dimensional unit existing in time and space. Though limited, within this system there is a greater degree of choice for theoretical movement.

Finally, Viola envisions a Schizo, or 'spaghetti', model in which 'not only are all directions equal, but all are not equal. Everything is irrelevant and significant at the same time'. The Schizo Structure is not based on a pre-ordered grid as in the Matrix, but is like a labyrinth or maze.

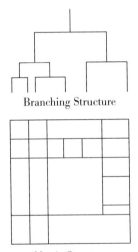

Branching Structure

Matrix Structure

Schizo Structure

L'Idea del Theatro has elements of all of the structures described above. It has a fundamental order based on the number seven: the Seven Pillars of Wisdom. Like Viola's Matrix Structure, this is multi-dimensional and exists within space/time. From this underlying order, images and ideas branch out. The image and ideas themselves are evocative and associative; they aim to trigger lateral thought.

The organic, branching patterns of an internet map really bare the closest resemblance to Camillo's idea. His divisions of imagery tend to proliferate in an uncultivated way. His data trees reproduce from stems that let loose, multiply, connect, and re-connect.

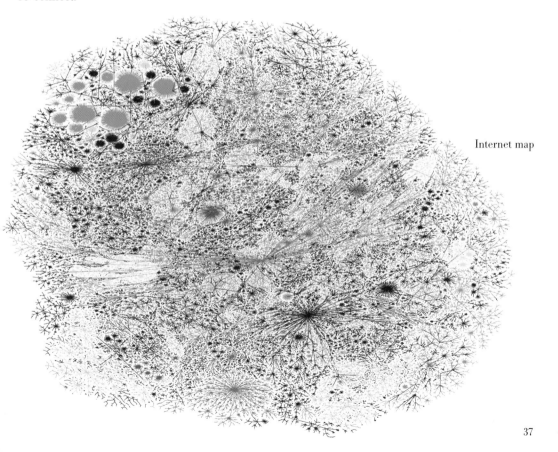

Internet map

To return again to Yates's description of the Theatre, one of the unusual, and important, aspects of her interpretation was that it reversed the typical relationship between subject and object. The object, or the 'perceived', was positioned in Yates's 'auditorium'. The subject, or 'perceiver', was positioned on the 'stage'. This is one reason why Camillo's work exemplifies so well Yates's theories on memory: the 'perceiver' would have a vast array of visual data from which to glean information. Yates's inversion of subject and object points to an inherently reflexive, subjective element of Camillo's work. There are two aspects to this. One is the subjectivity of the perceiver in terms of his place within the Theatre, and one is the subjectivity that is intrinsic to the visual experience.

The position of the subject, or perceiver, within the overall plan of Camillo's Theatre, is critical. It is from this position that everything else is witnessed. The entire pantheon is viewed from this spot. This is the centre of the subject. This is 'Me', the place of 'absolute reality'. Mircea Eliade has discussed how from ancient times, the sacred centre was the meeting place of heaven, earth and hell. As a mandala, or cosmographic representation, it was in the centre, that the universe was 'reproduce[d] . . . in its essence'.[38] From an architectural perspective, the centre of the sanctuary or temple, as the *imago mundi*, was the place of greatest significance. Inside Camillo's Theatre, the position of the centre is the place from which the network of visual relationships that surround it is to be understood. I shall discuss the relationship of the place of the centre to the rest of Camillo's Theatre further in Chapter 7.

The subjectivity intrinsic to the visual experience is difficult to quantify. In Camillo's *L'Idea del Theatro*, where the information field is encoded in complex visual signs, the meaning is, to an extent, dependent on subjective interpretation. While all information is dependent on context, the nature of visual information, in particular, is reliant on the frame. From our contemporary perspective, many of the Theatre's allusions – mythological, philosophical and visual – are distant. I don't think we can ever fully appreciate what Camillo may have meant by, for example, the myth of Pasiphae or the image of 'The Girl with Cut-off Hair'. But I do not think that it makes Camillo's message less valuable for being presented in a visual way. On the contrary, he understood the power of the image. But his visionary perspective meant he got embroiled in some knotty predicaments, such as those with his bookish adversary, Desiderius Erasmus, the turbulent relationship with whom I shall examine in the next chapter.

Chapter 3. Fame with Tongue
(Lingua verius quam calamo celebrem)

1431:	Lorenzo Valla writes: Philosophy 'is like a soldier or a tribune under the command of oratory, the queen', *De Voluptate*
?1469:	Desiderius Erasmus born
1470:	Pietro Fedra born
?1480:	Giulio Camillo born
1488:	Erasmus begins work on *Antibarbari*
1500:	*Adages* first published
1506-9:	Erasmus in Italy; meets Camillo, among others; Good Friday Speech, Rome (1509)
1516:	Publication of Erasmus's translation of the New Testament
1517:	Pietro Fedra dies
1520:	*Antibarbari* published
1527:	Erasmus's letter to Vergara regarding the paganism of the 'Ciceronians'
1528:	Publication of *Ciceronianus*
1530:	Camillo meets King of France who gives him funds for the Theatre
1531-2:	Zwichem's letters to Erasmus about Camillo – these are read and kept by Erasmus's secretary Gilbertus Cognatus; Camillo's *Trattato dell'Imitazione* circulates Paris and Padua in manuscript
1535:	Cognatus re-uses letter in which Camillo is mentioned

rasmus's *Adages*, first published in 1500, was a pan-European bestseller. For this collection of common sayings and proverbs, with explanatory notes, Erasmus culled his Greek and Latin sources, helping to immortalize such sayings as 'Know thyself', 'Put the cart before the horse', 'To be in the same boat' and 'To give someone the finger'. Some of the weightier adages, such as 'War is sweet to those who have not tried it', 'The Labours of Hercules' and 'The Sileni of Alcibiades', stimulated explanatory texts which ran to many pages and were published as separate pamphlets.

Erasmus revised and added to the *Adages* until it ran to over four thousand examples.[1] A handbook on how to flesh out your Latin prose with a meaty axiom, the *Adages*, like Erasmus's highly influential *De Copia*, became the standard work on how to achieve an 'abundance' of style. Often printed on cheap paper in numerous pocket-sized editions, it was handy, affordable, and it had a practical use. It helped you to look knowledgeable and in vogue – anyone who was anyone had a copy. Indeed, it incorporated so many revisions in new editions that it proved a source of endless interest and gossip.

Commentator, critic, author, wit and philologist, Erasmus was waspish, broad-ranging, curious, defensive, brilliant, restless and edgy. Born in Rotterdam and educated in Deventer, in the Netherlands, in 1469,[2] he refused to be hedged in; despite offers of remuneration and hospitality from kings and courts all over the Continent, he never settled. For periods, other than his native Holland, he stayed in England, Germany, France, Italy and Switzerland, dying in Basel in 1536. In his later years, his letters betray a preoccupation with his failing health, a desire for freedom above money, and, as in most of his work, a palpable sense of humanity.

Erasmus was a political animal, acutely aware of his own position, and of his effect, in relation to the world around him. He had to be. His translation of the New Testament into Latin, in 1516, though widely acclaimed, placed him at the very heart of the religious controversies of the age, and though he attracted wide-spread fame, he was equally criticized. Perhaps because of this, his voluminous and erudite letters to correspondents all over Europe reveal that he spent a lot of his time, when he was not laying the foundation for what he believed should be his luminous place in posterity, in looking over his shoulder. From the very beginning, Erasmus had been deeply embroiled in an emotional and ambivalent relationship to the Catholic Church – a tug of love and war that he battled with all of his life. It was with a mixture of admiration and suspicion that he was perceived by Church authorities.

This chapter is about Erasmus's *Ciceronianus*, a satire written in 1528 in which the name of Giulio Camillo plays a part. *Ciceronianus* raises several questions that are difficult to answer. There are questions of identity,[3] of reality versus fiction; and, crucially, about paganism. A pivotal speech is described in the book – the Good Friday speech – which may, or may not, have been a historical event and may, or may not, have been given by a Vatican librarian or by Giulio Camillo. Many commentators suggest that the orator was the librarian, Tommaso Inghirami of Volterra.[4] I will put the case instead for Camillo. This is not because the description of the speech flatters Camillo – as, we shall see, it doesn't! But I think that the book inadvertently gave a helping hand to Camillo's career. The publication of *Ciceronianus* came two years before Camillo's invitation to France. Ironically, it may have been *Ciceronianus* itself that helped to bring Camillo to the attention of the King.

Of course it may be that certain characters and events in the book were not *actually* based on any particular real occurrence or specific person but were composites, or fantasies, made up by Erasmus to make a point. Nevertheless, in a book a good third of which is explicitly concerned with an unambiguous, contemporary account of the literary and oratorical luminaries of the moment – with 'naming and shaming' – it does seem worthwhile to consider the hidden identity of those at its very core. It may have been that Erasmus's professed (rather than actual) assessment of Camillo was instrumental in undermining Camillo's reputation in the eyes of later historians, such as Tiraboschi and Bolgar.

I begin with a précis of *Ciceronianus* itself, with particular emphasis on the section regarding the Good Friday speech in which Camillo is named. Next I discuss the identity of the orator who gave the speech. I shall discuss the nature of Camillo's response to *Ciceronianus*, the *Trattato dell'Imitazione*. Lastly I shall look at the idea of paganism with regard to *Ciceronianus* and Camillo. Before any of this, however, I will attempt to put the idea of what was meant by 'Ciceronianism' in context.

Ciceronianism

The issue of Ciceronianism is a complex and broad-ranging topic. It was a debate that had rolled on for centuries, an ancient stylistic and ecclesiastical question. There were several strands to the argument: was Cicero the paragon of literary virtue or was that honour due to another? If he was a paragon, should we aim to emulate or imitate him or should we try instead to forge our own style? Was it, in fact, possible to create a literary style without reference to previous authors? And if it was necessary to refer to an earlier author then should that author be Cicero?

The debate became further complicated by the perceived lack of style of the authors of the New Testament. For the philologists, translators, commentators and critics whose job it was to deal in words, this question of style was paramount. And yet to be seen to align oneself overly with stylistics –particularly the sophisticated manner of Cicero – rather than to appreciate the writings of the New Testament as given and inspired by God, was seen as a victory of style over content and therefore worthy of derogation and ridicule: Ciceronianism became an open battlefield for irony versus piety.

By the early part of the sixteenth century, as the use of Latin and the vernacular in the universities vied for dominance, the issue of Ciceronianism got knottier still. Some of the so-called 'Ciceronians', for example Christophe de Longueil who is mentioned at length in *Ciceronianus*, were said to adhere to such a strict regard for Cicero that they aimed to imitate his every word and turn of phrase. Italy, as the homeland of Latin, and particularly the Roman Academy, was seen (justifiably or not) as the greenhouse of this particular strand of literary fanaticism. Cardinal Bembo, papal secretary to Leo X, was considered to be at the heart of Ciceronianism in Rome; his creed can be seen in a reply he sent to Pico on the subject: 'firstly, we must imitate the best models [i.e. the models of Cicero]; secondly, our aim must be to rival them; and, thirdly, in rivaling them, we must endeavour to surpass them'.[5] However, by as early as 1513, Bembo had already dropped the idea of one single model to imitate. Still others took a far more moderate view. As Levi says, 'The term 'Ciceronian' . . . covered a wide range of opinion and practice, and many a 'Ciceronian' was by no means as rigid and doctrinaire as [the] extremists caricatured by Erasmus'.[6] *Ciceronianus* itself, with its disparaging depiction of a 'Ciceronian' in action, did much to enflame the dispute. In fact the very term 'Ciceronianism' can be dated to the time of the publication of Erasmus's work.

Ciceronianus

Ciceronianus relates the imaginary conversation of the 'Ciceronian' Nosoponus (or Mr. Workmad), with Bulephorus (Mr. Counsellor) and Hypologus (his Back-up). Bulephorus aims to direct Nosoponus away from his narrow obsession with Cicero, in which endeavour of course, at length, he succeeds. The book can be divided, roughly, into three parts. In the first section, Bulephorus and Hypologus spy Nosoponus coming towards them, looking ill, 'more like a ghost than a human being'.[7] They decide to collude together to try to make him feel better, to cure him of his wasting Ciceronian disease, his 'style-addiction'. They engage him in conversation and Bulephorus himself pretends to be an adherent of Cicero and to share Nosoponus's infatuation, so that he will be allowed to become 'an initiate in the same mysteries'.[8] Nosoponus explains the lengths to which he goes to imbibe the full essence of his master: pictures of Cicero all over his house; not allowing himself to read anything but Cicero's works; leading a life of abstinence. He has prepared lexicons of the author's characteristic expressions and phrases in alphabetical order big enough for two strong packhorses to carry. The tone of this first section is light and bantering.

The second part of the story is heralded by the description of the Good Friday speech, which I shall return to later. From here on, the book turns serious. Bulephorus turns the table on Nosoponus; now he is 'in earnest'.[9] In several long speeches, Bulephorus gives forth on his theory that to be a Ciceronian is to be basically un-Christian: it is inappropriate for a pious Christian to be over-concerned with using Ciceronian language to discuss Christian themes; it has become the norm to value classical allusions over biblical ones, that to ape Cicero is to 'behave like a fool'.[10] Ciceronianism is, in short, says Bulephorus:

> ... paganism, believe me, Nosoponus, sheer paganism ...[11]

The third part of *Ciceronianus*, is devoted to a long discussion between the three main protagonists of who should be considered Ciceronian, and who should not. The characters trawl through Europe in a sweeping critical literary overview, which sent waves of scandal throughout Europe, sparking furious responses and wounding Erasmus's relationships.[12] In one of the most vitriolic ripostes Erasmus was accused of being culpable of nothing less than parricide, in defaming 'Our Father of Letters'.[13] Camillo, himself named in the book, also wrote a response, although it was mild in comparison. His *Trattato dell'Imitazione*, which I discuss later, circulated Paris and Padua in manuscript, but was not published until the year of his death.

Who Made the Good Friday Speech . . .

> In Rome at the time the two men with the most distinguished reputation as speakers were Pietro Fedra and Camillo . . . [14]

This is how the description of the Good Friday Speech begins, as the character of Bulephorus describes an impressive oration that he witnessed in Rome in the presence of the Pope. It is a long and uncomplimentary description. At the end he says:

> In short, this Roman spoke so Romanly that I heard nothing about the death of Christ . . . The only thing he could be praised for was for speaking in Roman fashion and recalling something of Cicero.[15]

Once Bulephorus has finally stopped talking, he is asked again for the name of the orator of the speech. He says:

> . . . I prefer to leave the name to be inferred, as it is not my present purpose to cast aspersions on anyone's name . . . the name of the man in my story does not matter . . .

But of course it does matter! *Ciceronianus* is hinged on the Good Friday speech. It comes at a pivotal point in the book, after which the tone and content changes from knockabout banter to critical deconstruction, not to mention the fact that casting aspersions on people's names is exactly what Bulephorus, Hypologus and Nosoponus then go on systematically to do.

. . . Pietra Fedra or Camillo?

Pietro Fedra was Tommaso Fedra Inghirami of Volterrra. Erasmus met and made friends with Fedra, by then a canon and Vatican librarian, in Rome, during his stay in the city in 1509. Erasmus mentions him in a letter to Joost Vroye (or Jodocus Gaverius).[16] In this long letter, Erasmus mourns the recent loss of their common friend, Jan de Neve. He says that he is feeling very mortal and goes on to talk about the people of distinction he has known in his life, throughout Europe, and the relative times of their demise. Pietro Fedra, he says, was under fifty when he died. He says that Fedra had earned his nickname by playing the part of Phaedra in Seneca's *Hippolytus*, in the piazza in front of the palace of Cardinal Raffaele of San Giorgio; that he was known as an authoritative orator. According to Erasmus, in fact, Fedra 'won more fame with tongue than with pen, for he was a wonderfully copious and effective speaker'.[17]

Twelve years after the letter mentioned above, when Erasmus was approaching his seventies, he wrote an autobiographical letter in which he makes reference to knowing Camillo.[18] If we take his letter at face value, it seems they were on friendly terms: he says he had actually shared a mattress with Camillo in Rome.[19] And there are other letters that show his interest in Camillo's work, as we know from correspondence between him and a man named Zwichem.[20] Zwichem, or Viglius Zuichemus, as he was otherwise known, was a lawyer, initially a disciple of Alciato. He met Erasmus in 1531, presenting him with a ring with the signs of the zodiac. Erasmus asked Zwichem to report to him on Giulio Camillo's work, and Zwichem was happy to oblige. Zwichem said that he met with Camillo in Venice and described

The Whirlpool of Artifice

the Theatre as 'a work of amazing character', 'with many images and caskets all over the place'. But it seems that Zwichem did not really understand what Camillo was talking about, and there are some incongruities in his account.[21] Nevertheless, the eventual fate of the letters is interesting. Erasmus's secretary at this time was Gilbertus Cognatus. Cognatus kept a copy of the letters from Zwichem and was later to pass them off as his own. Many years later, Cognatus used Zwichem's description of the wonderful Theatre in an imagined first-hand account. For Cognatus to bother to keep a copy of the letter for twenty-five years suggests that in private, Erasmus had shown a great deal of interest in Giulio Camillo. And whether or not we can believe the factual details of Zwichem's letters, one of Erasmus's replies reveals an interesting aspect of Erasmus's own opinion. In a letter written on 5 July 1532, Erasmus talks about Camillo's Theatre in terms, no less, of it being able to excite as great a 'tragedy in study' as that which 'Luther produced in religion'.[22]

Trattato Dell' Imitazione

Camillo's response was the *Trattato dell'Imitazione*. Written in Italian, it begins with an exhortation to Erasmus:

> What shall I say of you, Erasmus, man of so much knowledge and virtue . . . not only . . . eloquent, but also of good judgement?[23]

Camillo makes it clear that while his and Erasmus's views on imitation are different, they are not at odds. Erasmus advocates imitation based on equivalence of style, while Camillo recommends an imitation stemming from a judgement of, and identification with, the nature of the imitated. Camillo's tone is mellifluous; he aims to coax and please, and urges Erasmus to change his opinion:

> Turn, oh unique genius, change your style, and you yourself will be content to say the opposite of what you have written, if, as I believe, you feel the opposite.

48

In Camillo's opinion, there was once a golden age of language, or more specifically a 'golden century', and this was the century of Cicero. Language, like the rising and the setting of the sun, has a beginning, a zenith and decline, and it seems only sensible, in the light of this, to look to the 'most perfect time' for guidance for the creation of new language. This is not to say that every word and phrase must originate from here, as after all new concepts and new inventions require the creation of new words to describe them. Nevertheless, the guiding principles that informed the underlying structure of the language represented by the golden century should be adopted to achieve the best style and meaning. This is not to say that a new author should slavishly copy the old. Camillo makes the comparison between language and an ancient edifice. If an architect wanted to make a new building from old bricks, he would need to dismantle the old building and recreate it to his own design, using his own sense of judgement. This sense of judgement can be informed by the sense of beauty or balance of an old master, and yet the building itself will be wholly new because it has been re-constructed through the agency of a new vision. Rhetorical flourishes of the old style will still be visible, just as an architectural piece of cornice work, or a sculpture, may retain its form as an intact reminder of the old work, but still the overall work will be a new formation.

In many ways, Camillo and Erasmus do not diverge in their opinions, but say much the same thing, each from a different perspective. And as Camillo says in the beginning with his exhortation to Erasmus, he assumes that Erasmus himself is a man of 'good judgement' who needs only a little encouragement to admit that they share the same opinion. Only towards the end of the piece does Camillo venture a little anger, saying that he is willing to draw his sword to defend his own opinions; but, even at this point, Erasmus is himself not mentioned by name, and the episode feels very 'tacked-on', a very muted, if not tongue-in-cheek, rhetorical flourish.

Ars Oratoria

That Camillo wrote a response at all to *Ciceronianus* is the strongest evidence that he was implicated personally in the work. Tommasso Inghirami, or Fedra, of course, was not in a position to clear his name, having been dead for twelve years before Erasmus even came to write the book. Despite Fedra's distinction as the 'Cicero of his generation', is it possible that Erasmus has mentioned him in the context of the orator of the Good Friday speech as a (conveniently dead) red herring?[24]

It was as orators rather than as writers that men like Fedra and Camillo won renown. As Erasmus himself said of Fedra, he '. . . really won more fame with tongue than with pen . . . '. Fedra's written literary output is not substantial. Camillo's work was all in manuscript at the time that Erasmus wrote the work in 1528. It was thanks to Girolamo Muzio and others[25] that printed versions of Camillo's writings have survived at all. Camillo clearly was ambivalent about the power of print – an ambivalence that he shared with many others.[26] But perhaps this is where we are given a real clue as to why Erasmus chose these two men at all to illustrate his text: it was that their very threat lay not so much in the written, or printed word, as in their spoken word.

'Philosophy,' wrote Lorenzo Valla in around 1430, 'is like a soldier or a tribune under the command of oratory, the queen.'[27] Valla, whom Erasmus greatly admired, was instrumental in placing the idea of philosophy at the service of oratory and rhetoric, or the art of the word. Oratory, and orators, treated the question of ethics 'much more clearly, weightily, magnificently' than did 'the obscure, squalid and anaemic philosophers'. This ideal of eloquence was based on a belief in the persuasive power of the word: the very breath of the word itself an active agent of change.

Erasmus was by no means oblivious to the power of the word. But there was in Erasmus a tropism for the written, rather than the spoken word. It was in text itself, for him, that power resided. He may personally have had difficulty in expressing himself orally. As he said of himself, in a social setting, he was 'a man of few words, and do not push myself forward'.[28] He felt most at home in expressing himself not in speech but in text. Even in his *Adages*, proverbs designed for spoken use, '. . . though Erasmus is purportedly training a "speaker" or "orator", . . . the proverb seems most often to be found within the context of the written document'.[29] But there was more to Erasmus's antipathy to what he termed 'Ciceronian' than can be accounted for even by his insecurity over the spoken word.

Paganism

Despite what he was later to say in *Ciceronianus*, Erasmus's involvement and fascination with pagan authors had begun early in his life. Like Valla, his Italian precursor, one of his first missions had been to rid Europe of what he considered to be stylistic barbarians who did not appreciate the nuances of form represented by some of the pre-Christian writers. He began his major work on the subject, *Antibarbari*, in around 1488, when he was only nineteen years old,[30] adding to, and revising it, for over thirty years.[31] It was, for Erasmus, a seminal work. Like *Ciceronianus* it is written in the form of a dialogue between a number of characters who represent different positions in an argument. One of the characters, Batt, who, like Bulephorus in *Ciceronianus*, is thought most closely to represent the views of Erasmus himself, says:

> . . . For my part, I will allow myself to be called after any pagan so long as he was deeply learned or supremely eloquent; nor shall I go back on this declaration, if only the pagan teaches me more excellent things than a Christian . . . [32]

It was through his very appreciation of the gifts of the pagan that Erasmus was himself able to bring depth and colour to his Christianity. Erasmus was not alone in this of course. Pagan imagery and influence permeated culture from the new translations of pagan authors to pagan imagery in the visual arts. Painting and sculpture was awash with a sea of nymphs, fauns and satyrs. And there were subtle and powerful fusions of pagan with Christian theological motifs. Da Vinci's *Virgin and Child with St Anne*, for example, shows an image in which the positioning of the leg of the lamb across the knee of Jesus 'gives him the impression of a little hoof, like Pan, the spirit of awakened nature'.[33] Michelangelo's famous sculpture of Moses depicts him with horns radiating from his head.[34]

However this may be, Erasmus's position with regard to paganism changes radically around 1528. There are many reasons for this that are outwith the scope of this work to address but I think that two principal causes for the alteration are represented in the figure of Giulio Camillo. First, Erasmus's reputation was based on the printed word, and he viewed with suspicion those whose power lay in the spoken word; this was more than merely a difference in presentation, but crucial to the depth of persuasion which it was believed that an author or an orator could attain. Second, Erasmus was suspicious of developments in science, specifically the science propounded by Camillo. Camillo's image based system was a 'divine' philosophy: he was looking at the stars: an essential image of Camillo's Theatre, crucial to the idea of its spatial arrangement is Pan, the ancient god of the flocks. The magus in Erasmus believed profoundly in a philosophy based on the power of the printed word and he distrusted this vision of what he branded as a pagan cosmology.

'What I call philosophy', wrote Erasmus, 'is not a method of analysing first principles, matter, time, motion, infinity, but that wisdom which Solomon deemed more precious than all riches and on that account prayed God to give him above all else.'[35] While he is explicit about what he thinks philosophy is *not*, Erasmus is gnomic about what it *is*. It is not a branch of thinking that deals in matter and measure and time, in the first principles of Plato, or Aristotle, or Pythagoras. It is not about the exterior, material world. The implication is that wisdom is an internal, spiritual attribute; that philosophy is secret, God-given, precious. For all his rationalism, at the heart of Erasmus's philosophy is a recognition that wisdom is granted, not grasped, a free gift. Camillo and Erasmus shared this, at least, in common. To return to Erasmus's *Adages* with which this essay began – his great profusion and abundance of proverbs was not so very far from what Camillo achieved in a visual and spatial sense with *L'Idea del Theatro*. Where Erasmus created a bricolage of letters, Camillo intended a collage of imagery and myth. Where Erasmus intended to collate every known maxim throughout history, Camillo intended a visual scheme based on a systematic structuring of language. While Erasmus translated, interpreted and expounded his numerous sources, Camillo synthesized disparate philosophies. This is not to say that Camillo matched Erasmus as the seemingly rational thinker of the age, but that he possessed other knowledge that Erasmus wanted to undermine.

While Camillo was not, like Erasmus, a political animal, this is not to say that he was unconcerned with power. Harnessing spiritual, temporal and personal power was precisely what Camillo cared about and travelled Europe to advocate. Camillo shows us what matters to him in *L'Idea del Theatro* when he talks about the transformation of spirit and matter. Illusion, appearance, dissimulation, signs, visions and eternity are what interest Camillo, as well as the skill, Prospero-like, to interpret and orchestrate the symbols and attributes of the world. It is here, I think, that we begin to find the root of Erasmus's charge of paganism. For along with preaching the power of transformation, Camillo also talked about practical steps of how it could be achieved and this, as I shall discuss in the following chapters, was informed by a vision of a holy world animated by cosmic love.

Chapter 4

Hypnerotomachia Poliphili

n 1499, Aldus Manutius, the esteemed Venetian printer, broke with his long-held practice of publishing books of a purely scholarly nature, by printing an anonymous work of fiction called *Hypnerotomachia Poliphili*. Written in a mixture of vernacular Italian and invented Latin, it recounts the story of the dream of Poliphilo and the long search for his desire, embodied in the woman, Polia. The book is in two parts. The first is devoted to the dream pilgrimage of Poliphilo through the imaginary island of Cytherea in search of Polia, the climax of which is at the Fountain of Venus, situated in the very centre of the island. The second is mostly related from Polia's perspective and is set in the city of Treviso in north-eastern Italy.

The 1499 edition of *Hypnerotomachia Poliphili* has a warm red cover with a pattern of gold around the edge. The publication was so opulent in fact that Manutius himself, as well as the anonymous author, ended up out of pocket in the enterprise. The book is lavish with images. This is not only inherent in the text itself, as the landscape, layout, temples, statues and monuments of Cytherea are described in fantastic detail, but also in abundant pictorial woodcuts that represent and deepen the textual descriptions. In common with many of Aldus Manutius's books, the initial letter of each of the book's thirty-eight chapters is ornately decorated with patterns and knotwork. In 1512, a reader of *Hypnerotomachia* noted an acrostic made by these thirty-eight initial letters: POLIAM FRATER FRANCUSCUS COLMNA PERMAVIT (BROTHER COLONNA GREATLY LOVED POLIA). The reader then scribbled in the margins that the said Brother Colonna now lives in Venice at the monastery of Saint John and Saint Paul. The revealed identity of the author links

Elephant and Pyramid.
Hypnerotomachia Poliphili.

Hypnerotomachia to the Order of Preachers – the Dominicans – with whom Francesco Colonna was a lifelong friar.[1]

Hypnerotomachia Poliphili, as well as being a romance, was considered an excellent alchemical handbook. It was a very popular work and had a conspicuous effect in terms of its influence on visual and literary culture. Images from *Hypnerotomachia* – like the one of an elephant and a pyramid – caught the public's imagination and were to find their way into court pageants and festivals all over Europe. Images of an elephant and a pyramid are significant in Giulio Camillo's *L'Idea del Theatro*. But these are not the only correlations between the two books. I think that Colonna's *Hypnerotomachia*, itself a visual and verbal crossword, offers clues to the unravelling of Camillo's idea.

This, and the following chapter, will look at *Hypnerotomachia* to gain a greater insight into Camillo's *L'Idea del Theatro*. Direct influences can be traced from Colonna to Camillo in a number of striking visual, textual and theoretical correspondences. In this chapter I shall discuss Colonna and Camillo in terms of their relationship to emblematic and visual iconography. I shall look at two of their shared motifs: the elephant and the three-headed wolf, lion and dog, and discuss their respective significances within the text of each book. As mentioned above, the image of the elephant had a wide currency in Europe in the latter part of the sixteenth century, while the widespread occurrence in Italy of the image of the wolf, lion and dog, has been traced from the fourteenth century (though the origination of both images may be much earlier).

There is equivalence, in the economy of the *Hypnerotomachia*, between visual image and textual message. Colonna addresses and expresses theoretical ideas equally from a visual and a textual angle. His methodology provides a progressive, or evolutionary, interpretation of a given symbol or idea. Camillo uses this same technique of progressive interpretation, in a spatial sense, in the Theatre. Both authors favour a message from multiple viewpoints. These are expressed within, on the one hand, Colonna's pastoral and monumental, and on the other, Camillo's architectural and cosmological settings. I shall go on to discuss this in relation to the doctrine of the Topics and in terms of memory practices of the period.

Towards the end of the chapter I shall discuss the influence Camillo was later to have on emblem literature. *Hypnerotomachia* is cited as one of the visual antecedents of Alciato's *Emblemata*, while there is evidence that large sections of Camillo's *L'Idea del Theatro* were later used in parts of Valeriano's *Hieroglyphica*.

While there are interpretative similarities in terms of specific symbolic motifs, the two books are very different in their underlying structural form: Camillo's *L'Idea del Theatro*, discussed in more depth in Chapter 6, is a treatise based on the spatial description of a cosmic model, whereas the *Hypnerotomachia*, at least on the surface, is a fantastic linear narrative. Nevertheless, as I discuss in Chapter 5, both men, in their different ways, are aiming to express a similar vision – Colonna: visual and narrative; Camillo: visual and scientific. I have decided to look at these issues through the lens of Colonna's *Hypnerotomachia* not because the authors share similar motifs (though they do) but *because* of the difference of their textual forms.

Hypnerotomachia Poliphili

Hypnerotomachia begins with Poliphilo falling asleep beside a 'calm and silent shore'.[2] He dreams that he enters a frightening forest,[3] in which, among other things, he finds a pyramid, a colossus and an elephant, and is scared by a dragon. He escapes the dragon, and is met by the Nymphs of the Five Senses, who lead him into the realm of Queen Eleuterylida (or 'Free Will'). At Eleuterylida's castle he passes through the portals attended by Cinosia, Indalomena and Mnemosyna into the inner courtyard, where the walls are adorned with images of the planets. He journeys on in the company of Logistica and Thelemia and arrives at three doorways carved out of hewn rock. He decides to enter the middle doorway, named Erotrophos. He meets and falls in love with a nymph, who leads him on the rest of his journey. They witness the triumphs of Europa, Danae, Bacchus and Leda[4] processing past Jupiter. They enter the Temple of Venus where the High Priestess ceremoniously unites Poliphilo with his accompanying nymph, who was Polia all along. Two turtle doves and two white male swans are sacrificed from which 'a rose-bush grows miraculously with fruits and flowers'.[5] Poliphilo, Polia and the High Priestess taste the fruit. Poliphilo goes to look at some ruins and an ancient temple, before Cupid arrives in a boat to take him, and Polia, to the island of Cytherea. Poliphilo describes Cytherea: a perfectly circular island divided by rivers, meadows and hedges of orange, citrus and myrtle. He tells of the 'Procession of Honour in which Cupid was seated on the Triumphal Vehicle, and Polia and Poliphilo followed, bound together; and they came with great pomp to the gate of the marvellous Amphitheatre'.[6] He describes 'the wonderful artifice of Venus's Fountain in the centre of the Theatre, and how the Curtain was torn and he saw the Divine Mother in her majesty'.[7] Mars arrives and they leave the Theatre, coming at last to the tomb of Adonis, Venus's beloved.

Joscelyn Godwin, Francesco Colonna's translator into English, says that the language of the *Hypnerotomachia* 'is so strange and idiosyncratic that there is truly no parallel to it in literature. It could probably only have been forged at this particular time, in a climate of linguistic uncertainty'.[8] Colonna managed to combine Italian syntax with a Latin vocabulary in a work that even Godwin says at times is unreadable. Colonna (like Camillo) has had his fair share of detractors. Recently, for example, Simon Schama (1995) described Colonna's language as mediocre, while Yates dismissed his work as a 'wild imaginative indulgence'.[9] While the style of Colonna's prose may leave something to be desired and lightweight as *Hypnerotomachia* may appear (in content rather than form – the book is nearly five hundred pages long), it has also stimulated more generous responses. Jung, for example, discussed the work in terms of its connection to memory and archetypal imagery.[10] A recent blockbuster, *The Rule of Four* (2004), has used *Hypnerotomachia Poliphili* to create not only a mystery thriller but also an interactive web-game!

The language of *Hypnerotomachia* is interesting from a purely historical perspective in terms of Colonna's manipulation of Latin with Italian. Camillo devoted much of his time to noting and charting vernacular differentiations in the region of the Veneto, and himself chose to write in Italian, though he does not go so far as Colonna in creating an individualistic or idiosyncratic language. Colonna pillaged from *De architectura* of Vitruvius and Leon Battista Alberti's *De re aedificatoria*, to help embellish the lavish descriptions he gives of architecture, monuments and gardens, though, as Godwin says, while *Hypnerotomachia* 'may be a landmark in the history of architectural writing . . . it is not the manual of a practitioner.'[11] Many of these architectural motifs were to find there way into the work of Camillo as I shall discuss further in Chapter 5.

Hypnerotomachia is steeped in wordplay. The title itself is an amalgam of three Greek words: *hypnos* (sleep), *eros* (love), and *mache* (strife). The protagonist's name, Poliphilo, means 'lover of many'. The first named encounter is with Queen Eleuterylida, or 'free will' and subsequently Poliphilo meets a succession of allegorically named characters. The list of allegorical characters itself reads like a poem-pilgrimage through a sensual and moral landscape, beginning with free will and ending with Algerea, or 'sorrow-bearer', the servant of Diana's Temple.

An example of Colonna's textual use of the sign, along with its visual equivalent, can be seen in his description of the base of the sculpture of the elephant and pyramid, mentioned at the beginning of the chapter. It is given here in full as it offers a good flavour of the language of the book. Poliphilo says:

. . . I saw the following hieroglyphs engraved in a suitable style around the porphyry base. First, the horned skull of a bull with two agricultural tools tied to the horns; then an altar resting on two goat's feet, with a burning flame and, on its face, an eye and a vulture. Next, a washing basin and a ewer; then a ball of string transfixed by a spindle, and an antique vase with its mouth stopped. There was a sole with an eye, crossed by two branches, one of laurel and the other of palm, neatly tied; an anchor, and a goose; an antique lantern, with a hand holding it; an ancient rudder, bound up together with a fruited olive-branch; then two hooks, a dolphin, and lastly a closed coffer.[12]

Poliphilo then explains that the 'hieroglyphs' that he has just described in the text were 'carved in the following graphic form' and this image is inserted into the text:

Hieroglyphics.
*Hypnerotomachia
Poliphili.*

Colonna then provides us with an interpretation of these 'ancient and sacred writings'. He says:

FROM YOUR LABOUR TO THE GOD OF NATURE SACRIFICE FREELY. GRADUALLY YOU WILL MAKE YOUR SOUL SUBJECT TO GOD. HE WILL HOLD THE FIRM GUIDANCE OF YOUR LIFE, MERCIFULLY GOVERNING YOU, AND WILL PRESERVE YOU UNHARMED.

My own breakdown of the interpretation of each of the hieroglyphic images follows. (Obviously my interpretation of the hieroglyphic images has been influenced by Colonna's textual translation of, or key to, the system. Nevertheless, once provided with the key to the internal logic of the hieroglyphic system, subsequent examples of the code become much easier to decipher – which presumably Colonna intended in the first place.) The animal's skull is sacrifice, the agricultural tools, labour. The altar with the goat's feet is the altar of the god of nature, represented by the feet. The eye, the burning flame and the vulture show that it is being tended, guarded and watched. The washing basin and ewer shows the purification of the soul. The string transfixed with a spindle shows the guiding principle of god in the long and winding ways of life (a similar motif appears in Camillo, incidentally, when he talks about garments constructed from a 'mass of unworked wool', though, here Camillo is discussing the creation of the earth). The antique vase with its mouth stopped, old memories and grudges, stilled. The sole with an eye shows that the follower will be led in the walk of life by the guidance of god, the laurel and palm show that this will be victorious and peaceful; the anchor linked to the goose, the hand to the antique vase and the rudder to the fruited olive branch show that all paths through life, present, past and future are well balanced and guided. The hooks may be symbolic of capture, perhaps capturing the following images. The dolphin and the coffer represent the god of the sea and the fullness and richness of the earth as well as the unknown.

It should be noted that this is only the inscription on the base of the sculpture of the elephant. The significance of the elephant itself, with the obelisk on its back, is not explained by Colonna in the text – which, of course, is not to say that they do not have a symbolic meaning. Colonna has several 'categories' of symbolic motifs, some of which he interprets textually, and some of which he leaves as purely visual signs. The example above, of the text, hieroglyphs and interpretation at the base of the sculpture, comes early in the book. Colonna has put it here, I think, so that the reader is prepared to imbue the rest of the visual images in the book with the same degree of interpretative depth.

The visual elements of Colonna's narrative could be said to fall into several broad categories: hieroglyphic signs like the one above; visual representations of ancient text; descriptive 'pictures' of action; drawings of architectural monuments or features.[13] All of these distinctions overlap – hieroglyphic or emblematic motifs find their way into 'pictures' for example[14] – but I think that it may be a useful distinction to make in terms of Colonna's influence on Camillo. Aside from their mnemonic function, each one of these visual elements provides a subtly different function within the story. Representations of ancient text turns the text itself into an image. Representations of action, like a cartoon strip, fulfil a narrative function. Hieroglyphs have their own inherent specific iconographic grammar. The distinction between the meaning inherent in a hieroglyph and in other visual iconographic systems (and in what the distinction between these are in the first place) opens the gates to a vast semantic field which it is outwith the scope of this work to discuss. It also begs the question of how, and in what way, the experience of meaning is changed from a textual and a visual perspective. Colonna's work – as an example of the liminal place between text and image – is, I think, in this respect, extraordinary.[15]

Colonna's narrative cannot be understood without reference to his visual grammar. Visual signs are to be understood, to be 'read', in the same terms as text; the reading of the hieroglyphs and visual motifs is an integral part of the story itself: it moves the story on in time. We cannot get from point A to point B without taking into account the importance – the literal significance – of the image. Colonna is not content to express an idea from one viewpoint, using not only text and image but also, as in the example above, the interpretation of the image itself. This approach reinforces the fact that he intends there to be a progressive element to the interpretation of visual and textual signs. The image has 'plot-value'. Likewise, we need to understand Camillo's images in terms of their significance over time. Camillo's images are not static like butterflies pinned on a board. He adopts a similar system to Colonna of progressive interpretation of an image. In the Theatre, ideas, in graphic form, are presented from multiple viewpoints. The same image may appear at a different place within the Theatre and therefore be imbued with a subtly different meaning. In a sense, images are invested with 'compound interest' as they appear at different positions within the system. Camillo's treatment of the image of the elephant, which he shares with Colonna, exemplifies the structure.

The Elephant

The elephant, 'the most religious animal of all the beasts'[16] is described at two levels in the Theatre: on the outermost, at the level of Prometheus and at the level of the 'simples', the Banquet. At the Banquet Camillo says the elephant signifies 'the origin of the mythical gods' while at Prometheus, it represents 'the religion of the mythical gods'. The level of the Banquet is where the two essential productions of God originate: the 'eternal' word, and 'primary matter' which is 'in time',[17] while the outermost, or Promethean, level of the Theatre is 'assigned to all the arts,

Elephant at the level of the Banquet.
The most religious animal of all the beasts . . .

Prometheus	X
Sandals of Mercury	
Pasiphae	
The Gorgons	
Cave	
Banquet	X
Planet: Mercury	

The position of the two occurrences of the elephant image in the Theatre, at the levels of the Banquet and Prometheus. They are both on the Mercury column.

noble as well as vile',[18] as discussed in Chapter 2. The image of the elephant appears under the influence of Mercury, messenger of the gods, and the planet that 'appertains to . . . language and the telling of tales'.[19] Religion, therefore, root and flower, is to be understood as a part of language. The progression represented through the levels of the Banquet to Prometheus, is a gradual gradation from nature to art, essence to artifice, from idea to human skill. When the elephant is represented, its significance evolves according to its position. At the level of the Banquet it represents the being, the origin, or source, of the gods, while, at Prometheus, it represents the human show, or manifestation, of the origin, in religion.

Elephants are mentioned in the *Hieroglyphics* of Horapollo. Aldus published this in 1505, six years after his publication of *Hypnerotomachia*. Camillo may well have been influenced by the work of Horapollo, but I think that Camillo's interpretation of the elephant is closer in fact to Colonna's. Horapollo describes the elephant in terms of a 'A Powerful Man [who] knows what is Right', or in the case of an elephant and a ram: 'A King that flees from Folly and Intemperance'.[20] Horapollo's elephants are more concerned with temporal power than Camillo's version. Camillo's interpretation of a religious animal is nearer to Colonna's enigmatic representation.[21]

The Wolf, Lion and Dog

Camillo and Colonna share the image of the three-headed wolf, lion and dog, which represents time: past, present and future. Camillo explicitly equates the image with what he terms 'Saturnine' time. I think it is useful in the terms of this image to understand Mircea Eliade's distinction, within 'archaic ontology', of what he calls 'profane' and 'mythical' time.[22] (Eliade's definition of what constitutes 'archaic', or 'primitive', is itself based not only on what has happened in the past, or in history, but in what he perceives as man's innate response to 'being'.[23] He gives an example of the 'mythicization' of an actual histori- cal event – the expedition against Poland in 1499 by Malkoš Pasha – in which almost nothing of the facts of the case were preserved in the ensuing historical ballad but were transformed instead into 'mythical action'.[24] He provides a number of fur- ther case studies up to the twentieth century.[25]) Profane time, according to Eliade, is situated in history; it is unrepeatable and linear. Mythical time, on the other hand, situated outside his- tory, is renewable and transcendent. The tendency throughout the Middle Ages and beyond, which gained increasing adher- ence, was what Eliade called the 'immanentization' of the myth- ical theory, which survived 'beside the new conception of linear progress'.[26] Mythical time, unlike 'linear progress', was capable of 'resumption . . . from the beginning, that is, a repetition of the cosmogony.' He cites the Saturnalia and other examples of ritu- alistic events that denoted 'a repetition of the mythical moment of the passage from chaos to cosmos'.[27]

Wolf, lion and dog at the level of the Cave. *Illustrate the three times . . .*

Camillo's and Colonna's respective images of the wolf, lion and dog are best understood in terms of 'mythical time'. Eliade's distinction between a time that is common, linear and quanti- fiable and a time that is common, mythic, and immeasurable is helpful, here. Camillo explicitly makes a similar comparison between the time that is represented by the relationship of the Earth to the Sun, which is quantifiable, to the time represented at the level of Saturn, which is a more complex, and in a sense, more introvert relationship. For both authors, the image of the wolf, lion and dog represents the subjective form that time takes; it is not days, minutes and hours as they are generally measured, nor even the seasons, but internal time, measured in experience and memories. It is the time of the 'interior man'.

Just before Poliphilo and Polia reach the culmination of their journey, they take part in a fabulous 'Procession of Honour', when a 'numberless host of demi-goddesses bearing gifts and

Triumph of wolf, lion and dog.
Hypnerotomachia Poliphili.

noble nymphs of especial beauty trooped up . . . with a great display of ornaments and pomp'.[28] Each of these gifts and displays is meticulously described, and several are shown as drawings. The final display, carried with 'especial devotion and resolute awe'[29] shows the three faces of a wolf, a lion, and a dog; the image was Egyptian in origin, denoting the monstrous animal that accompanied the god, Serapis. Knowledge of the animal was brought to the attention of a Western readership through Macrobius's *Saturnalia*, in which it is mentioned:

> **Next to the god a huge, strange monster sits . . .**
> **On the right it looks a dog and on the left, a grasping wolf;**
> **Between a lion. A curling snake**
> **Joins these heads: they mean the passing times.**[30]

An early appearance of this image was in the frontispiece to Franchinus Gaforius's *Practica Musicae* printed at Milan in 1496. This Allegory of Music shows a picture of Apollo with a lyre seated on a throne above the tail of a long winding snake. The snake descends through an Aristotelian layer of fixed stars, the planets, and levels of fire, air and water to the earth itself, in which it culminates in the faces of a wolf, a lion and a dog. The implication is that eternal divine influence is imparted to the earth through the aegis of present, past and future time.

In Camillo's Theatre, there are three representations of the wolf, lion and dog image all of which appear under the influence of the planet of Saturn. They appear on the levels of the Cave, Pasiphae, and the Sandals of Mercury. Camillo specifically names Macrobius as his source for the image, saying that Macrobius wanted to 'illustrate the three times, that is, the past, present and future'. He says:

> **. . . the wolf signified time past, because he has already devoured it**
> **. . . the lion is the present . . . because present troubles thus encountered, strike terror in us, which the face of a lion would do if it overcame us . . . the dog indicates future time, because in the manner of a fawning dog, the future always promises us something better.**[31]

The interpretation of the image changes as it moves through the different levels of the Theatre. At the most basic, or elemental level, that is: at the Cave, it represents Saturnine time, in general. 'Saturnine time' is discreet from 'solar time'. Solar time is quantitative; it is calculated by the 'nearness or distance [of an object] from the sun . . . [or] by the course of the sun'. The seasons, the hours, the minutes and the years are dictated, therefore, by the Sun. (It is significant that Camillo should choose the Sun as the unit of measurement of linear time, rather than the Moon. The Moon, in its cyclical periods, had for centuries been commonly used as the basis of time measurement. In 1514, however, as deliberations for calendar reform were underway, issues regarding the respective positions of the Sun and Moon to the Earth were critical.[32]) Camillo's description of Saturnine time suggests a more personal, subjective experience, than solar time. In discussing the life-cycle of an organism he talks about the 'length of time the union of the mixed stay together', bound by spirit, until 'dissolution'[33] (in other words, the length of time in which the elements of an organism are alive); this is Saturnine time. It is based on an individual's consciousness, rather than the collective need for a common reference point, it is a feeling rather than a coordinate.

At the level of Pasiphae, Camillo states that the image of the wolf, lion and dog is differentiated to mean 'man being subject to time'. We know that this is Saturnine, rather than solar time. This means that we should not interpret 'man's subjection' to time in the sense of clock-watching, or measurement, but rather in organic, less quantifiable terms, such as the ebbs and flows of relationships (relationships in the broadest sense, from the microcosmic level to macrocosmic). Moving on to the image under the Sandals of Mercury, Camillo says that the image is to do with delaying and postponing and bringing things to an end. Now, it signifies the propensity within human beings to slow down or to cease relational activities.[34] At each position the

Prometheus	
Sandals of Mercury	X
Pasiphae	X
The Gorgons	
Cave	X
Banquet	
Planet: Saturn	

The wolf, lion and dog image appears on the levels of the Cave, Pasiphae and the Sandals of Mercury, all of them on the Saturn column.

emphasis of interpretation has changed. At the Cave, the focus is on the planet Saturn's relationship to the concept of time. At Pasiphae, where the agency of man is brought into the equation, the emphasis has shifted; now it is about the felt experience of Saturnine time from the perspective of the inner man. At the Sandals of Mercury, where the Theatre has gone one further step away from spirit towards matter, the emphasis is on the procrastinatory effects of Saturnine time on the activities of man.

Colonna's image of the wolf, lion and dog appears in a
picture of a great triumphal procession. It is significant that the
image should appear at such an important place in the Colonna
narrative. The procession has taken twenty-one pages to
describe; the wolf, lion and dog is the final image to be explained
before the 'triumphant host' arrive at their destination, where
they pass through a portal created by the 'spraying [of] scented
water'[35] and are admitted into the presence of the great Mother

Opposite and above: Triumphal Procession. The image of the wolf, lion and dog is in the panel directly above.
Hypnerotomachia Poliphili.

Goddess, Venus, where the arrows of her divine son, Cupid, wound Poliphilo and Polia's hearts. Why would Colonna put the image of the wolf, lion and dog here, at this pivotal point? Could it be that the hero and heroine have reached a place where Colonna wishes the whole of time to be represented? The linear aspect of Poliphilo and Polia's journey has come to a point of culmination: they have reached their journey's end before the final revelatory ritual. The sign of the wolf, lion and dog shows that this should be understood not only in terms of the linear progress from the thicket in the woods to the temple of the gods, but also in terms of the protagonists' subjective, internal journey from confusion to clarity.

I hope that in these examples it is clear that for both Colonna and Camillo the interpretation of an image is dependent on its relative position within the rest of the schema as a whole: either Colonna's narrative structure, or Camillo's Theatre. Both authors rely on interpretative progression for their message; in a sense, the images' interpretations are space and time dependent. Chapter 5 will look further at some of the pastoral and monumental motifs that are shared by Colonna and Camillo. But now I shall discuss their work in terms of the tradition of the topics, and of mnemonic systems. The final part of this chapter will look at ways in which Camillo and Colonna may have contributed to later emblematic literature.

A Trained Memory

On one level, Camillo's and Colonna's images can be understood in terms of memory systems. The source for the practice of memory systems can be found in a number of ancient texts: Cicero's *De Oratore*, parts of the *Rhetorica ad Herennium*, (an anonymous textbook, from around 86-82 BC, thought erroneously in the medieval period to be by Cicero), Quintilian's *Institutio*[36] and Aristotle's *Topics*. Before the advent of print, the use of a trained memory was understandably deemed to be a useful tool. Thomas Aquinas went so far as to make it a moral necessity, saying that it was an attribute of the virtue of Prudence.[37] One ancient mnemonic system, variations of which have survived up to the present day, suggests the technique of visualizing objects in a dramatic way. In the 1980s, Tony Buzan's adaptation of old and familiar mnemonic methods was made popular with a BBC television series and accompanying book that promoted aerobics for the memory,[38] for example.

The text from the *Rhetorica ad Herenium*, from which Buzan and others' twenty-first century enthusiasm may, circuitously, have evolved reads:

> ... if we set up images that are not many or vague but active; if we assign to them exceptional beauty or singular ugliness; if we ornament some of them, as with crowns or purple cloaks, so that the similitude may be more distinct to us; or if we somehow disfigure them, as by introducing one stained with blood or soiled with mud or smeared with red paint, so that its form is more striking, or by assigning certain comic effects to our images ... that, too, will ensure our remembering them more readily...[39]

The advice in the *Rhetorica ad Herenium*, confirmed by Cicero's *De Oratore*, was adapted over the years into an architectural mnemonic system in which a building was imagined, inside which, in different rooms, or beside particular pillars or corners, statues or other striking images were placed to give visual aides to the memory. The building was the stable element in the scheme, while the images inside it could change according to the thing that was being remembered. The architectural mnemonic was in vogue until around the first century AD when it 'declined in popularity and was considered cumbersome and gimmicky'.[40] It then made a spectacular comeback in the thirteenth century with endorsements by both Thomas Aquinas and Albertus Magnus. The name of the Dominican Order, of which Aquinas and Albertus were luminaries, often appears in relation to the creation of mnemonic systems throughout the medieval period and into the Renaissance, although the Franciscans and other Orders were also active in the field. They devised not only architectural mnemonic systems, but others that relied on numerical or alphabetical grids, or on visual imagery. Yates goes so far as to discuss the paintings on the walls of the Chapter House of the Dominican convent of Santa Maria Novella, in Florence, in terms of memory images, as well as Giotto's representations of the virtues and vices in the Scrovegni Chapel at Padua.

Aristotle's doctrine of the topics was central to medieval philosophy and is also important in understanding memory practices of the period. The *topica* have been called 'the construction material for thoughts'.[41] Dialectical arguments were based on the topics. It was only through dialectic that 'a true and infallible knowledge of the world' could be obtained, while the efficacy of subjects such as mathematics, for example, was suspect.[42] In Greek, a topic was called a *topos* and in Latin, a *locus*. As Green-Pederson points out, the *topos*, or *locus*, was not an easy thing to define: literally it meant 'place' but it could also mean 'commonplace', or, sometimes, 'topic'.

According to Aristotle, a trained memory 'will make a man readier in reasoning', as he will have facts and relevant logical stages of an argument at his mental fingertips. The utility of the two hundred images described in Camillo's Theatre, therefore, is twofold. On the one hand, as memory aides, the images encapsulate ideas for further exposition (this is the view of the Theatre, as expressed by Frances Yates).[43] On the other hand, the images are stages within a reasoned proposition, the interpretation of which is dependent on the image's precise position within the overall schema, as discussed above. The particular space that an image occupies within the Theatre will affect the interpretation and meaning of the image itself. A recurring image will alter in meaning subject to its position and the surrounding influences.

A correlation can be seen in *Hypnerotomachia*. The narrative logic of the book is expressed by the progress of the protagonist, Poliphilo, through a symbol-laden landscape. The significance of the symbolic-images is subject to the place and time that it occurs in Poliphilo's journey. Likewise, for Camillo: the narrative logic of his proposition is expressed through the place and time that an image occurs in the Theatre.

In her wide-ranging account, Yates looks at mnemonic systems from the classical period, and assesses Camillo's *L'Idea del Theatro* in this light. Camillo's descriptions of imagery certainly fulfil Yates's definition of good memory images; but I do not think they should be regarded as the *point* of the book. Each image is imbued with meaning and points the way to further exegesis. But it is the overall structure and the relationships between the images on which Camillo concentrates his focus, in *L'Idea del Theatro*. While mnemonic techniques were known and used by Camillo as a useful tool, it is not the subject of his book. The very concept of Camillo's 'Theatre of Memory', in fact, is Yates's own. In Camillo's *L'Idea del Theatro* he discusses his *idea*. The Theatre itself has no name.

In studying the proliferation of mnemonic techniques during the medieval period, it is sometimes easy to forget that mental gymnastics were not the point of the exercise. They were merely means to an end. Mary Carruthers has talked about memory practices in terms of '"thinking about" and for "meditating upon" and for "gathering"'[44] while Neil MacGregor discusses the paintings at the Dominican convent of San Marco in Florence not as memory aides, (nor even 'principally as objects of beauty') but as 'visual instruments of instruction'.[45] MacGregor analyses Fra Angelico's depiction, at the convent, of the Crucifixion in this light. Showing Dominic, the founder of the Order of Preachers, at the foot of the Cross, 'The scene is bare, with only sky-blue for background, and no other participants but ourselves.' MacGregor goes on:

Fra Angelico has not pictured an anecdote from the life of St Dominic any more than he has painted the actual Crucifixion . . . what is shown is the object of Dominic's prayerful meditation. We are allowed to see what he sees in his mind's eye . . .[46]

MacGregor subsequently discusses an example of a Franciscan devotional booklet from around 1330-40. This tiny ivory and gold inlaid book shows scenes from the Passion. The final four panels present the 'hieroglyphic reminders' of the *Arma Christi*, two of which are seen opposite.

'Thousands upon thousands' of examples of the *Arma Christi* have survived, suggesting that Western Christian uses of hieroglyphs was widespread and well established when Colonna composed the *Hypnerotomachia*. What MacGregor reminds us is that the purpose of these images, although they served a mnemonic function, was primarily didactic and inspirational. They were a starting point for meditation, an inward journey, a 'solitary, mental walk'.[47]

The inspirational or meditative aspect to symbolic imagery is further discussed with regard to Colonna and Camillo in Chapter 5, when I look at the revelatory quality inherent in their sign systems. The final part of this chapter is devoted to their influence on emblematic work.

Emblems

Though neither Colonna's *Hypnerotomachia* nor Camillo's *L'Idea del Theatro* can really be termed an 'emblem book', as such, each had a significant effect on later emblematic work, and both rely absolutely on the use of signs, or hieroglyphs, in order to get their message across. A large part of *L'Idea del Theatro* became incorporated in an important emblematic work: Valeriano's *Hieroglyphica*. This, like much of Camillo's story, came about in a roundabout and unusual fashion. It appears that Camillo's work was used, after his death, by a

number of former students and associates passing it off as their own. Wenneker has shown that sections of Allesandro Citolini's work, *La Tipocosmia* (Venice,1561), are identical with passages from Camillo's *L'Idea del Theatro*.[48] There are parallels between both books in terms of their overall theme and the title of Citolini's work suggests that Citolini primarily understood Camillo's work through the auspices of cosmology and science. The cosmological aspect of *L'Idea del Theatro* is further explored in Chapter 6. Significant as this may be, *La Tipocosmia* is not an emblem book. However another associate of Camillo's, Agostino Curione, was also involved in the plagiarism of his work, which led directly to elements of the text of *L'Idea del Theatro* being inserted into the compilation which became known as Valeriano's *Hieroglyphica*. The 1567 Basel edition of Valeriano's *Hieroglyphica* includes two additional volumes by Celio Agostino Curione. A significant number of the images in the additional volumes of the *Hieroglyphica* are directly attributable to Camillo. Twenty-two of the emblems in the first volume are inspired by Camillo, and at least five of the emblems in the second additional volume are by him, while another nine more use the same images as appear in Camillo although their interpretations are different.[49]

Another link can be found in the woodcuts that accompany the *Hypnerotomachia*. These, like the text of the work itself, were published anonymously. A number of the images reappear in a later emblem book: Achille Bocchi's *Symbolicae quaestiones* . . . (Bologna, 1555). The hieroglyphic images reproduced earlier, for example, make an appearance in Bocchi's work as an emblem dedicated to the mysteries of Egyptian letters.[51] Other elements, though modified, such as the animal skull,[52] processional triumphs[60] and architectural motifs[53] are also re-used. The artist credited with creating the woodcuts for Bocchi's work is Giulio Bonasone, from Bologna.[54] it is on record that Giulio Camillo and Bocchi were themselves acquainted: both attended a special council created in Bologna – 'Il Concilio per il Volgare' – to discuss modifications and developments in the Italian language.[55] Bocchi's *Symbolicae quaestiones* itself contains an emblem specifically devoted to Camillo, the image of which is reproduced in this book in the Epitaph. There was clearly a close personal and philosophical connection between these northern Italian writers and artists who saw the subversive potential of encoding a message within an image.

Chapter 5

Revealing Venus

'the visual act always
precedes the act of loving'

Dante, *Paradiso*[1]

espite its complex storyline, there is, in *Hypnero-tomachia*, a great deal of humour. In fact, one cannot read it without suspecting that the entire thing is an elaborate joke. Colonna writes much of the narrative with his tongue in his cheek as he describes his wanton, frolicking nymphs and almost permanently aroused Poliphilo. Even when the hero reaches the innermost sanctum of the great goddess at the climax of the book, he is brought out of a wide-eyed reverie by rudely stubbing his erring toe on the polished obsidian floor. This is not to belittle the book, or, paradoxically, to make it a less serious work. The innate jokiness of *Hypnerotomachia* is important. Camillo, on the other hand, is not so prone to laughter. But this reflects the different approaches and textual forms of the two books. *L'Idea del Theatro* is designed to analyse space – it is a technical work. *Hypnerotomachia*, at least on the surface, is a good yarn. Nevertheless, there are strong resemblances in terms of their philosophy, their underlying chord.

Synonymous with the visual and sensual element of *Hypne-rotomachia*, is the belief, for Colonna, in the power of eroticism, or, rather, of seeing the world through the eyes of Eros. On one level, the book reads as a straightforward dream of romance. But on another, it can be seen as an allegory of love, sacrifice and renewal dramatically played out in a world in which all that is represented is holy. Eroticism, or the interplay between seduction and temptation, giving and receiving, at the level meant by Colonna, anticipates the basis of the scientific theories of which Camillo was an advocate, in which every atom of the universe is sacred, awaiting the influx of the life-giving 'celestial streams' and 'spirit of Christ'.

The motif of beautifully decorated curtains, or veils, is reiterated at key points in Colonna's narrative. The opening, or tearing, of the veils is a necessary prerequisite for Poliphilo's, and eventually Polia's, revelation of Venus, the mother goddess, in all her naked beauty, at the heart of the story. The idea of veils leads us back to Camillo who begins *L'Idea del Theatro*:

> **The oldest and wisest writers always have had the habit of protect-
> ing in their writings the secrets of God with dark veils, so that
> they are understood only by those, who, as Christ says, 'have ears
> to hear', that is, those who are chosen by God to understand His
> most holy mysteries.** [2]

He continues by saying that Moses, after returning from the mountain and his encounter with God, 'could not be looked upon by the people, unless he covered his face with a veil'. And then, later: 'upon seeing Christ transfigured, that is, almost separated from the grossness of mankind', the Apostles were only able to comprehend Him through 'signs and visions'. For Camillo and Colonna signs, by definition, were riddles, sphinx-like and sacred, to be understood only by lifting aside the veils, which conceal them.

In this chapter I shall explore how the themes of eroticism and creation are expressed respectively in *Hypnerotomachia* and *L'Idea del Theatro* in terms of revelatory images. It is difficult to talk about revelatory imagery without reference to memory practice. Certain images, such as the *Arma Christi* mentioned in Chapter 4, were seen as having inherent power. By reminding the viewer of the divine, they stimulated a divine response, a 'starting point for meditation', the contemplative beginning of an inward event. The revelatory quality to some of Camillo and Colonna's visual imagery bypasses text. Their works *rely* on visual sense-experience for meaning. This is non-discursive; and is outwith, or deeper than, rationality. The use of images provides a kind of 'super-text' to the whole. There are differences to the ways that each author adopts the use of this super-text. At the most

basic level, Colonna, for example, uses images like a construction manual, while at other times they are wholly enigmatic. I think that Camillo, on the other hand, believed that it was under the aegis of the image that comprehension and understanding – that revelation itself – was possible.

In *The Book of Memory*, Mary Carruthers talks about the 'continuous understanding' of Dante's angels in *Paradise*.

> **From the first moment these beings found their bliss**
> **within God's face in which all is revealed,**
> **they never turned their eyes away from It;**   78
>
> **hence, no new object interrupts their sight**
> **and hence, they have no need of memory**
> **since they do not possess divided thought . . .**[3]   81

The face of God 'in which all is revealed', found in the Empyrean Heaven, is the consummate image for the angels. No beauty or wisdom can compare with it; it is their deepest desire. As the angels' contentment is complete, because their vision of god is immanent and immediate, they 'have no need of memory' because they are only aware of the present moment; the past (and the future) is not relevant. While angels 'have no need of memory', Carruthers continues, humans, on the other hand, must 'know by remembering physically-formed phantasms'.[4] The idea of the *physical* impression of images on the memory is derived from Thomas Aquinas's interpretation of Aristotle. An image 'is not ghostly like that of a photographic slide projected on a screen, but is an actual physical imprint that permanently affects the brain tissue . . . The change in the eye occurs in the same manner in which phantasms are recorded in memory, like a seal in wax.'[5]

In this chapter I look at a number of shared motifs that address the corresponding themes of eroticism and creation that I believe are essential to both *Hypnerotomachia* and *L'Idea del Theatro.* I shall focus on three that particularly embody the matter: these are the significance of flowers, a map, and the Theatre. There are a number of other similarities, but these ones in particular address the themes above. In a sense, however, the key similarity is that they both move seamlessly between reality and myth. For both authors, the possibility of revelation – the possibility of looking deeply into things to find a mythical dimension – is exposed in the everyday. The real, material world has as much valence as an imaginary, allegorical universe; while on the one hand, Camillo uses mythological motifs and symbols to describe material reality, on the other, Colonna uses the real world to embellish his myth.

Godwin has suggested that the 'Temple to Diana' (of which the character of Polia is a devotee) represented in Book Two of *Hypnerotomachia* is a convent in the modern city of Treviso, and that Polia herself represents a real woman with whom Colonna was in love. Like the Monastery of Saint John and Saint Paul in Venice with which Francesco Colonna was associated for most of his life, the convent associated with the austere church of San Nicolò, which still dominates the skyline of Treviso, is also Dominican. Should we presume, then, that the 'real woman' that Colonna was supposed to have loved was herself a Dominican nun at San Nicolò? Was their relationship a *bona fide* love-affair? Or should we instead understand Colonna's 'Temple to Diana' as a purely allegorical symbol, even if it was based on a truly existing place? Is Polia really a fictional character? As allegory, she is all beauty and truth; as real woman, she is a red herring? From the outset, the veracity of *Hypnerotomachia* in terms of the identity of the author, and the nature of the allegory that it contained, has provoked more questions than concrete answers.

Even if there will never be definitive solutions to questions of identity in *Hypnerotomachia*, I still think that Colonna can help to unravel the maze of Camillo. They still share underlying similarities in terms of their factual experience, and their internal subjective projection, of the world. Both share and express an experience lived on the brink between reality and myth. I shall look further at the subjectivity that is at the heart of the visual experience in the final Chapter. But perhaps their particular emphasis on the cross-over between truth and invention can be ascribed in part to the specific culture from which they came. Venice, with its maze of alleyways and waterways, canals and tunnels and bridges is a contradictory city. A cobbled path becomes moving water; a bridge is a meeting place; a vast colonnaded square turns into the turquoise Adriatic.

As we shall see, the similarities between *Hypnerotomachia* and *L'Idea del Theatro* in terms of spatial orientation and cosmic arrangement are further pronounced as regards their shared central motif of a Theatre, and I shall discuss this further at the end the chapter, but I would like to turn now to their shared focus on the significance of flowers.

In flowers, says Camillo, 'lies the secret of all the secrets that it is not permitted to reveal'.[6] He is talking about one of the most enigmatic of the symbols of the whole Theatre: the ark of the covenant.[7] The ark, says Camillo, 'signifies the three worlds', that is, the supercelestial and the celestial worlds, and 'this lower world', which is exposed to heat and cold and 'all the changes'. He places the ark on the level of the Cave, under the influence of Saturn, in other words he sees it as an 'elemental' symbol under the influence of Saturnine time. Camillo regards the ark itself as giving 'place' to all things that are contained in the three worlds, while the 'meanings' of the worlds have been assigned to Pan (who, as I discuss in the following chapter is possibly representative of the Earth). That the ark is concerned with 'place', under Saturn, suggests that we should understand this not so much as a geographical location, as in terms of temporal, historical, mythical position. The ark, as the container of the mysteries of the worlds, is located at Saturn, while the interpretation, or meaning, of the mysteries is revealed by Pan.

Ark of the Covenant at the level of the Cave.

Venice, *c*.1600.

In describing the celestial world as represented by the ark, Camillo says that it is, itself, symbolized by a 'candelabra of gold with seven lamps signifying the seven planets'. (Whether this candelabra and the following images are actually inside the ark itself is not clear.) A 'separate lamp with three arrows by its side' symbolizes the Sun 'in its superiority'. There are 'some vases' which represent the reception that the planets experience from the 'supercelestial influxes'. 'Spherical figures' indicate the planetary spheres. And then we come at last to the flowers, which hold the deepest secrets and greatest mysteries. Their significance is such that even here, in *L'Idea del Theatro*, when he has finally agreed to reveal the secret of the Theatre to Muzio, after fifteen years of keeping silent, the mystery known only to the King of France, he is unwilling, or unable, to divulge the meaning of the flowers. Flowers are connected to time, to a representation of the spiritual essence of God manifested in tangible reality. Transient, rooted in the earth and dependent on the heavens, flowers are reminders of the macrocosm within the microcosmic. Perhaps they are also representative of the receptivity and openness that is required to receive the influx of the supercelestial.

For Colonna, flowers are everywhere. Flowers adorn the riverbanks, are worn by the nymphs, make garlands for the triumphal processions. Fields and meadows are filled with wild flowers; there are formal knot gardens, trellises and palisades of flowers. The scent of flowers fills the air. There is even a miracle of flowers at the Temple of the High Priestess.

Poliphilo is symbolically united with Polia at the Temple of the High Priestess, in a ceremony that prefigures their vision of Venus. The ceremony begins with a sacrifice of two turtle doves and two white swans. The Priestess scatters the ashes of the swans onto a large urn in the centre of the temple, from which instantaneously appears a miraculous rose bush laden with red

Polia, Poliphilo, the High
Priestess and the Rose Bush.
Hypnerotomachia Poliphili.

Diana and the Garment
at the level of the Cave.

fruit. The Priestess picks three of the fruit, giving one each to Poliphilo and Polia to eat, and eating one herself. After eating the fruit of this miraculous rose, Polia reveals to Poliphilo that she has been a devotee of the same Order as the High Priestess; however, with the High Priestess's blessing, Polia, metaphorically speaking, casts aside her veil, and instead devotes herself to Poliphilo. Their symbolical marriage, allows them their later vision of Venus; it is as a united pair, as man and woman joined, that they are granted their greatest revelation within the context of Poliphilo's dream, as a whole. This, as we shall see, occurs in the centre of the island of Cytherea.

The Map

Poliphilo's journey is punctuated with descriptions of architecture and monuments, processions and pastoral scenes, nymphs, satyrs, centaurs, gods and goddesses all described in minute detail, in 'close-up'. The story itself almost reads like a continuous series of *tableaux vivants*. If Colonna had filmed his epic rather than written it, one senses that he would have used a macro lens for the entire work, focusing on skin, hair, leaves, flowers, as though they were only a breath away. Occasionally he draws back for a wider perspective, as when, for example, he describes the layout of the Island of Cytherea, and reminds us of the sense of progression in Poliphilo's journey. But any sense of urgency to arrive at his goal is tempered with, and occasionally almost overwhelmed by, his sensuality, that revels in the experienced, the present moment.

Cytherea itself – a 'delightful and pleasant island' – is the goal of Poliphilo's expedition. It is perfectly circular; a mile in diameter. The island itself is made up of a series of ever contracting circles of meadows, groves, and fields, all subdivided in a radiating pattern. A river, beside an ornate peristyle that encircles the island, is banked with narcissi, hyacinths, lilies,

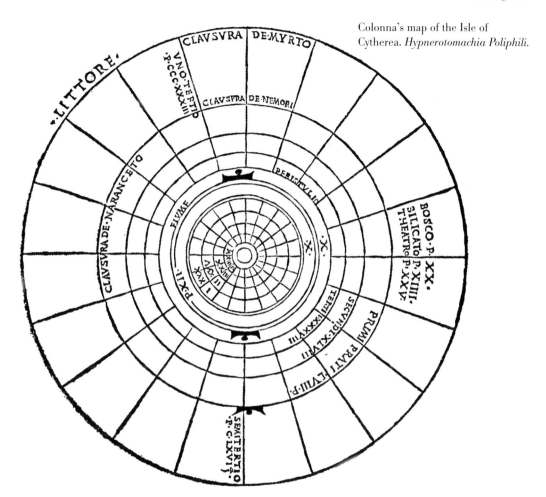

Colonna's map of the Isle of Cytherea. *Hypnerotomachia Poliphili.*

gladioli, marigolds, dandelions and violets. The outer circles contain cypress, myrtle and citrus trees. The mid section is made of formal circuits of fields, each divided into little square gardens. The interior part has knot gardens, gardens with emblems, mosaic pavement and marble paths; there are orange, myrtle and box hedges, stairs and colonnades.

The map of the island is the only perfectly circular motif in the book, and Colonna tells us how it is precisely subdivided into gardens and enclosures: 'The first garden was 33 paces, the second 27 and the third 23 . . . the wood was 25 paces wide . . .',[8] and so on. I shall return to the description of the island shortly, but I would like to make a little diversion, here, to describe an earlier architectural motif in the book. This is the palace of the Queen Eleuterylida (Free Will), from which, with the Queen's blessing, Poliphilo had set out on his mission to find Polia near the beginning of the story.

The Palace of Free Will.
Hypnerotomachia Poliphili.

After passing through a curtain held by the lady Mnemosyna (memory), Poliphilo had come to a 'spacious court . . . perfectly square'. Here, the walls were 'all covered with plates of pure, lustrous gold', and Poliphilo saw, 'with great pleasure [that] the seven planets with their innate qualities [were] perfectly represented'. There were also 'seven triumphs of the subjects ruled by the planets . . . the seven harmonies of the planets, and the transit of the soul receiving the qualities of the seven degrees'. All of the 'celestial operations'[9] were depicted with accuracy and skill. We are led to understand that the metaphysical is represented, here, with precision. The Queen's throne, itself, was located at the place of the planet Sol, 'raised above the others'[10] because of its importance.

Eleuterylida's palace is interesting in a number of ways. First, it is significant that it is Mnemosyna, or memory, that should open the curtain to reveal the scene. Within the economy of the story, memory, here, is similar to a part of Camillo's conception of the three intellects of the interior man. Memory in this instance can be understood not only as a memory for facts, for tangible data – for things outside oneself; but also, in the Thomist or Dantesque sense as a deep, interior memory in reception of the 'divine ray'.[11] Mnemosyna has *revealed* the vision to Poliphilo, her action of moving aside the veil has actively allowed him to move deeper into the palace, to witness the scene. She has revealed a picture of interior space. Allegorically speaking, the respective gender of the protagonists – of Mnemosyna and Poliphilo – is essential to the active and passive roles that they embody, as are all the gender roles in the book. The disclosure provided by memory allows the protagonist to enter an interior and metaphysical space in which he encounters the personification of free will, which is positioned at, and emanates from, the place of Sol, associated with the Sun. This metaphysical space can be understood at the level of an interior personal space and at the level of an interior projection of cosmic space. It is microcosmic and macrocosmic.

At the level of the interior personal space, then, Poliphilo, at the palace of Eleuterylida, has come to a place where he is given a vision of inner freedom. 'no treasure in the world could possibly compare with that which you truly find in me,' says Eleuterylida. 'neither the almighty Creator nor orderly Nature herself could have shown you a greater treasure than to reach my divine presence and ample munificence'. Free will itself, says Eleuterylida, is a 'celestial talent veiled from mortals,'[12] but she bestows on Poliphilo the opportunity to experience it fully. That this gift should be bestowed in her palace, surrounded by representations of the planets, suggests that this can be understood, at the level of projected cosmic space, in terms of planetary influence; that in a sense the power of Eleuterylida has freed Poliphilo from the effects of astrological determinism.

I have made this long diversion from the island of Cytherea to make the point that Poliphilo's journey can be understood in terms of a number of spatial levels: there is interior personal space and interior cosmic space.[13] These are the allegorical or 'deep' spaces of the book. There is also the level of the evident, explicit, linear storyline, which could be called the 'shallow' space of the book. It is the tendency of the book as a whole to flit between these shallow and deep spaces which I think is one of the reasons that *Hypnerotomachia* seems humorous – the reader is never certain whether Colonna is in 'deep' or 'shallow' mode.

When Poliphilo and Polia come to Cytherea to find the fountain of Venus, their entrance is a cosmic enactment of the union of free-will and love. This can be understood, as discussed above, at the allegorical level of the 'interior' man as a ritualistic and mimetic enactment, but it can also be recognized as a representation of real cosmic space. Godwin points out that Colonna's work fits 'within a long tradition of "cosmic" interiors, beginning before the book was written with the astrological decorations at the Palazzo Schifanoia in Ferrara, and culminating in the seven planetary rooms originally planned for the palace of Versailles'.[14] His work was to have a significant affect on later garden design, for example at the Villa d'Este, the Venus Grotto at the Boboli Gardens and the Sacred Wood of Bomarzo.[15] Echoes of the island garden of Cytherea can be seen in the Botanic Garden at the University of Padua, as I discuss below. There is no reason to suppose that *Hypnerotomachia*, although written in the form of a romance, was not also interpreted in the light of a practical manual. Colonna's influence, then, in terms of Camillo, becomes one not only of emblematic or symbolic motifs, as discussed in the previous chapter, but also of the physical arrangement of landscape and space.

For Camillo, Venus is represented by 'a sphere with ten circles'. Like Colonna and the description of Cytherea, Camillo's sole emphasis on circularity appears here, at Venus. The tenth circle, he says, 'shall be golden and full of spirits', with a 'volume' that appertains to the 'Elysian Fields and the souls of the blessed'.[16] He says that, here, also 'the earthly paradise' will be discussed. These subjects have been assigned to Venus 'because of the delight and charm of such places.'[17] The connection was synonymous for Camillo with the idea of circularity, an 'earthly paradise' or garden, and the planet of Venus. The similarities between Colonna's motifs for Cytherea and Camillo's representations for Venus here are conspicuous. And the similarities in terms of planetary arrangement and cosmic space do not end there. Their most striking correspondence is in the use of the motif of a Theatre to describe the most sacred – the most divine – sanctum of all.

Venus at the Banquet . . . *golden and full of spirits.*

The Theatre

A wood of rare trees surrounds the innermost part of Cytherea, reiterating the first wood from which Poliphilo had originally stumbled to begin his journey. This time, however, rather than a place of fear and confusion, the wood is a:

> . . . blessed, happy, comfortable and leafy wood where streams of bright water [rush] through little channels and winding rivulets, and sacred springs [run] with a soporific murmur . . . here, beneath the shade of the young leaves, there echoed many a lively conversation as countless noble nymphs sequestered themselves . . . [18]

The Amphitheatre.
Hypnerotomachia Poliphili.

The nymphs, elegantly dressed in 'thin silken crêpe' in a variety of pastoral colours from saffron, swan-white, yellow and yellow-green, interspersed with the occasional violet, 'sang to antique instruments and busied themselves . . . with rustic pursuits' while in the trees, 'strange and beautiful birds, never before known or seen by the human eye' were 'intent on their love-making, hastening with delightful chirping through the branches that were modestly clad with bright and never-falling leaves'. Beyond this sylvan scene, stairs lead to an 'impressive colonnaded enclosure [that] formed a wall around a spacious site, separate, unimpeded and flat . . . decorated with a marvellous creation of emblematic mosaic'.

> . . . in the outmost triumph, the magnificent procession gradually approached an archway containing an open door conspicuous both for its material and for its workmanship, which led to a marvellous amphitheatre, built very high and filled with ornaments of art and artifice, the like of which was never seen . . .[19]

The Theatre on Cytherea is 'exquisitely made and perfectly finished'. It is surrounded with flowers: myrtle and roses spill from flower boxes; there is a latticework of trees – cypress, box and juniper. The 'zenith of architectural ostentation', more than human, rather it is 'divine'. If the whole of Poliphilo's journey has been through a symbolic land of allegory, now that he has come to the centre, he is at the ultimate place of transformation and change.

The magical entrance way – 'a stupendous work; built of oriental lapis-lazuli'[20] – leads to the interior, where 'at first sight [Poliphilo thinks he is] witnessing a most stupendous miracle'.[21] Here, a smooth expanse of black stone appears to be the deepest abyss as well as the cloud-filled sky. Poliphilo imagines that he is about to fall, only to be shocked into finding that he is looking at an illusion of the firmament.

> . . . the entire pavement of the arena . . . seemed to consist of a single, solid obsidian stone of extreme blackness and indom-

itable hardness, so smooth and polished that at the first step I
withdrew my right foot, fearing that I was about to fall into an
abyss and perish in the midst of all my love and happiness. But
its resistance soon brought my scared and shaken spirits to their
senses, by hurting the erring foot. In this clear stone one could see
the limpid profundity of the sky perfectly reflected as in a calm
and placid sea, and likewise everything around or above it, much
better reflected than in the shiniest mirror . . .

Colonna himself seems to be unsure how to describe the significance of the Theatre on the island of Cytherea. 'The astonishing Temple of Ephesus, the Roman Colosseum, the Theatre of Verona and all the rest must give way before this structure' he says. Is it a building designed for religion, for temporal power, for entertainment?

Theatre itself was going through a period of radical change at this time; how much Colonna was influenced by, or himself influenced, this transition is a moot point. It has been shown, for example, that Niccolò Perotti's *Cornucopiae*, which was published in 1489, may have had an effect on Colonna's work.[22] Perotti's *Cornucopiae* also uses the motif of a theatre. In Perotti's case it is an 'Amphiteatrum Caesaris'; he even has a temple to Venus. Perotti, like Colonna and Camillo, favours the use of emblematic material: the first thousand pages of *Cornucopiae* are made up of 'Epigrams' of varying lengths.[23] However even though there are obvious similarities, Perotti's emphasis in the *Cornucopiae* is more on temporal, rather than spiritual power.[24] His temple to Venus is an attribute of Caesar's Amphitheatre, rather than the end and goal to which the whole of the book is aimed.

Yates has correlated Camillo's Theatre, on the other hand, with the theatrical designs of Sebastiano Serlio, whose influential *Libro d'Architettura* was published in Paris in 1545. Serlio's designs for theatre were profoundly to affect the work of Palladio and his stage settings were to be copied for centuries. Parts of the *Architettura* sound as though they are describing

Camillo's *L'Idea del Theatro*. In the Theatre, says Serlio, we are made to watch as:

> **the horned and lucent moon rises slowly . . . In other scenes the sun rises, moves on its course, and at the end of the play is made to set . . . With like skill gods are made to descend from the skies and planets to pass through the air.**[25]

Serlio continues by discussing the place of the vanishing point in a theatrical setting in order to achieve the maximum appearance of pictorial depth, as I discuss further in Chapter 7. But it is debatable whether Camillo was influenced by or rather, himself, had an influence upon the architect.[26]

Perotti, Serlio and Colonna, as well as, of course, Camillo, each represent a different contemporary approach to the newly emerging *ideas* of Theatre. For Perotti, the Theatre is a symbol of political power. His Amphitheatre harks back to the antique days of the rule of Caesar, a time when Rome held sway in a military and economic sense and the Empire was great. Perotti's Theatre is first and foremost a literary metaphor – a concept – rather than an actual building. For Serlio, on the other hand, whose specific designs for Theatres and their internal settings deal in real space, it is a tangible, public building in which illusions can come alive; the Theatre is primarily a place of entertainment and distraction. Both Colonna and Camillo's Theatres deal in the divine and, to differing degrees and in different ways, the arrangement of cosmic space. Colonna marks out the Theatre as the locus of a kind of personal religious experience, a place of sensual and heavenly revelation. Giulio Camillo projects the idea of the Theatre onto the entire universe: the Theatre, for Camillo, is where man's relationship to the cosmos is understood.

The world's first Anatomy Theatre was built at the University of Padua in 1582. Inside this elliptical arrangement students crammed in to watch the dissection of bodies exhumed in secret from the city's graveyard. Although it was forbidden by the Church, staff and students alike ignored the ban in the

Model of the Anatomy Theatre,
University of Padua.

hunger to look inside the drama of the body itself. In an upstairs
room at Padua University, dedicated to Hieronymous Fabricius,
the Professor of Anatomy who initiated the Theatre, a row of
skulls is still kept – *memento mori* of the staff who donated their
bodies for the new science.

The design of the Anatomy Theatre at Padua was as much to
do with prosaic necessity as aesthetics. The tiered arrangement
allowed the students, who had to stand shoulder to shoulder
throughout the dissections, to physically support each other,
in case of nausea or fainting. The fascination with the inner
workings of the human body pre-dated the Anatomy Theatre

itself by decades. Camillo talks about witnessing the controlled disintegration of a body in *Trattato dell' Imitazione*. He says that he saw 'an excellent anatomist once, in Bologna, [who] enclosed a human body in a box full of holes'. The box was then 'exposed to the current of a river, which decomposed and destroyed within a few days all the flesh on the body, which then exposed of itself the wonderful secrets of nature, surviving alone in the bones and nerves.' He equates the flesh and bones of the body with a 'model of eloquence', which he says is sustained by 'matter and design alone'.[27]

The Anatomy Theatre at Padua shows that the design of theatres was by no means restricted to the use of a proscenium arch, or even that that the idea of Theatre was necessarily dependent on presenting an *illusion* of reality. The Theatre could equally be a place in which the outer layers of things could be stripped away to look at the truth of what lay beneath.

The first Botanic Garden in the world was created in 1545 also at the University of Padua.[28] It is in a circular enclosure that radiates out from a central fountain in neatly divided parterres, reminiscent of Colonna's description of the island of Cytherea. It is home to some of the oldest rare plants in Europe. Here, for the first time, this garden of 'simples', was adopted by a University. The study of herbal recipes for the cure of the body became a scientific drama in its own right. The plants themselves took centre stage.

Inside Colonna's Theatre the hero and heroine find the 'mysterious fountain of the divine Mother'.[29] Made from the same black stone that surrounds it, the fountain has a wall a foot high, 'heptagonal in its outward form and round within'. On the instructions of Cupid, Poliphilo tears aside a curtain brocaded with flowers, inscribed with the word 'Marriage', in the centre of the fountain, revealing Venus. The goddess is half submerged in water, her 'divine body . . . luminous and transparent . . . blazing . . . in the rays of the sun'.[30]

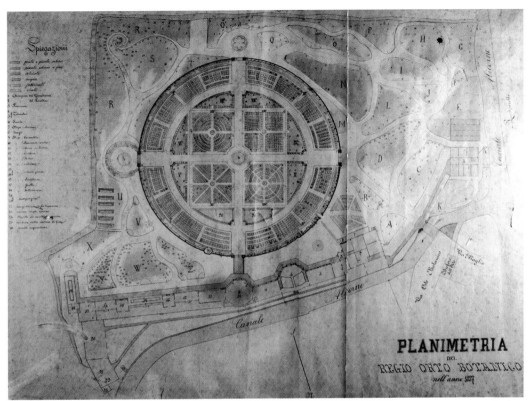

Orto Botanico, Padua.

The image of Venus waist high in water, in a sense, sums up Colonna's philosophy. The liminal place between appearance and manifestation, at the surface of things, is where meaning itself is exposed. And yet even though the goddess – the goal and summation of the journey – is a vision of complete beauty and love, she is still just out of reach. She is revealed and concealed, reflected and refracted, by the water of the pool. She is both immanent and remote. It is only the blood-letting of Cupid's arrows that allows the final denouement. Fluid, in a constant state of metamorphosis, Poliphilo's journey involves continuous

Fountain, Orto Botanico, Padua.

change, from one place to another, from one emotional state to another. The Theatre, finally, is where all Colonna's deep and shallow spaces converge.

Camillo's use of the Theatre as an overarching motif in which to draw a picture of his astronomical theories derives, in part, I think, from a similar philosophy to Colonna. Poliphilo is unable to operate within the context of Colonna's world without being wholly affected by the visceral experience of outside stimuli: '. . . not a single capillary but was penetrated by the amorous flame' says Poliphilo in describing the piercing of his breast by Cupid's arrow, 'while I seemed to be changing my form accordingly'.[31] In the same way, Camillo describes an animate world in which the plants, rocks and flowers are alive, in sentient reception of heavenly influence. For Camillo, 'celestial streams' operate on the earth from the heavens. These streams, as will be seen in Chapter 6, move through the very capillaries of the skin, of every single hair of man.

Chapter **6** **Divining Stars**

The very hairs of your
head are numbered.

Luke 12:7

arning the epithet 'divine' was not, for Giulio Camillo, a judgement of his personal qualities. It was simply because he looked at the stars.[1] Following in the footsteps of the Dominican scholar, Marsilio Ficino, Camillo believed that the Sun, which 'fosters and nourishes all things . . . is the universal generator and mover'.[2] Like Ficino, Camillo is usually perceived as a literary scholar and he has most often been judged in relation to those who deal in words. But Camillo's aim, his universal picture, is one that intimately combines the principles of natural philosophy, astronomy and number with mythology and language in a way that is markedly more systematic, or 'scientific', than Ficino. While the language that Camillo uses is based on art and mythology, his thinking is rooted in scientific principles that bear direct corellation to other Renaissance astronomical theories of the day. There are useful comparisons to be made between Camillo's *L'Idea del Theatro* and astronomical treatises such as the celebrated *Sphera* of Sacro Bosco, Pontano's *De Rebus Coelestibus* and even aspects of Copernicus's *De Revolutionibus*. Understood in the light of his scientific contemporaries Camillo's connection to Giordano Bruno may become clearer. This is an area of Camillo's work that has been passed over in recent scholarship,[3] while it is possible that for his contemporary detractors it was this very area – his science – that was misunderstood, to the detriment of his later reputation.

In 1517 the Paduan philosopher, Agostino Nifo went so far as to dismiss Ptolemaic theories as 'old wives' tales'.[4] The discovery, for the Europeans, of America by Columbus in 1492 had radically affected the mental map of the earthly world. By 1497, the Bolognan Professor (and tutor of Copernicus) Domenico da Novara, was propounding new theories for the heavenly one. Novara questioned Ptolemy's *Geography*, which for centuries had been for mapmakers a touchstone, as revered as Ptolemy's cosmological work, *The Almagest*, engendering a number of alternative theories in the ensuing decades. A contemporary account of these by the Jesuit astronomer and mathematician, Christopher Clavius, identified at least five different schools of cosmology in evidence in Italy alone as late as the seventeenth

Ptolemy's *Geography*

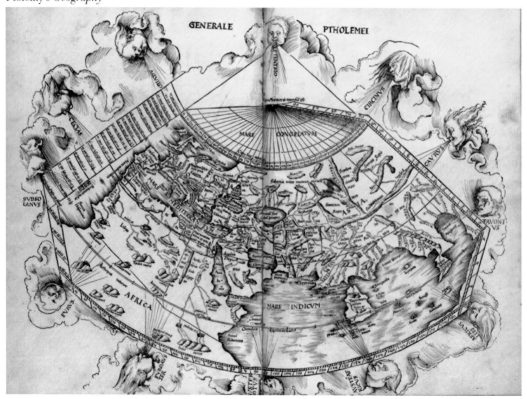

century. Nevertheless despite the plethora of alternative cosmologies, the prevailing orthodoxy held by the majority to be
correct at the turn of the sixteenth century was still generally
Aristotelian and Ptolemaic.

In order to place Camillo in his astronomical context, I
shall explore the scientific milieu from which Camillo evolved,
and make comparisons between his work and the ideas of his
contemporaries. I shall begin by looking at the Aristotelian
Ptolemaism of medieval Italy. This will necessarily be a very
cursory picture of a large topic, yet I believe it will be helpful
in order to understand Camillo's perspective. I shall outline the
basis of other – heterodox – contemporary cosmological theories
in evidence in Italy, namely the homocentric, 'fluid heaven',
'celestial channel' and Copernican theories. I shall make specific
comparisons between these hypotheses and aspects of Camillo's
L'Idea del Theatro. Finally I look at the innermost level of
Camillo's Theatre and discuss his theories regarding cause and
effect and the arrangement of the Sun, the Earth, and the other
planets, which are at the core of Camillo's hypothesis.

The Principle of the Spheres

The cosmological picture inherited by medieval Europe was
derived from the teachings of the Greeks and the Egyptians,
represented respectively by Aristotle and the astronomer and
mathematician Ptolemy.[5] Following Aristotle the medieval
world-view placed the stationary Earth at the centre of a series
of spinning spheres that contained the elements and the planets. Closest to the element of the Earth itself were the spheres
that contained the other elements: water, air and fire, in that
order. A fifth, superior, element called ether was the medium of
the heavens. All of the elements were subject to change, apart
from ether, which did not change but was in a state of endless
movement. Cicero, in *De Natura Deorum*, describing the nature

Interior of the dome of the Baptistery, Padua Cathedral. Giusto de'Menabuoi.

of ether (and quoted by Camillo in *L'Idea del Theatro*) says it is a celestial fire, 'tenuous, transparent and suffused with a uniform heat'.[6] In the ether, were the spheres of the Moon, the planets, the Sun and the stars.

Representations of cosmology ranged from simple linear diagrams in manuscripts or printed form to major works of art woven into the fabric of social and religious life. The interior of the dome of the Baptistery at the Cathedral of Padua, for example, painted by the Florentine artist, Giusto de' Menabuoi, at the end of the fourteenth century, incorporates an example of a Christian Aristotelian cosmological map.[7] The Earth is surrounded by concentric circles of colour. These represent the spheres that contained the elements that were thought, in accordance with Aristotle, to encircle the Earth, and the other planets. The outermost circle is surrounded by the signs of the zodiac, beside which, in a blaze of gold sits Christ with a bevy of angels. Above the head of Christ (not shown) is a perfectly symmetrical heaven crowded with saints, angels, God, Mary, and doctors of the church.

Heavenly depictions were not confined to Italian painters. Completed approximately a hundred years after de'Menabuoi's depiction at Padua, Hieronymus Bosch's translucent orbs in *The Garden of Earthly Delights* are probably a close visual equivalent to what was imagined by the term 'heavenly sphere', itself.[8] Bosch's '3-D rendering' shows how complex and delicate the visualization of the spheres could be, as well as illustrating that the spheres themselves, like Russian dolls, could fit inside each other. The most basic maps simply show a series of concentric linear circles, with a layer of 'fixed stars' at the outermost rim. The concept of a sphere was often ambiguous, and the boundary of each of the spheres was not clearly defined. Theories about the number of the spheres varied. But the most frequent model, shown for example in the popular astronomical treatise of John of Sacrobosco (written during the thirteenth century and used up till the seventeenth) showed the Earth surrounded by the

The Garden of Earthly Delights.
Outer panel. Hieronymus Bosch.

spheres of the elements, extending through the spheres of the
Moon to the planets and the Sun, to the sphere of fixed stars
The outermost sphere described by Dante in his astronomical
work, *The Banquet*, was called the *primum mobile*; this was
thought to revolve at immense speed, instigating the movement
of the spheres below it.[9] Outwith the *primum mobile* was the
unmovable Empyrean Heaven.

The movement of the spheres and the planets was thought
to be in perfect circles. However, according to Ptolemy the
pivotal point of the spinning of the planets and the Sun was on
its own 'deferent' orbit.[10] This 'off-centredness' was to account

Diagram of the Universe from
Peter Apian's *Cosmographia*
(Antwerp, 1584).

for the precession and recession of the planets in their yearly
orbits around the Earth. It was perceived that the planets
tended to look at times as though they were moving backwards,
and that sometimes their light was dimmer than at others, so it
was assumed that their motion must in some way be irregular.
Ptolemy's solution had for centuries seemed to solve the problem,
and his extensive tables of star data and planetary predictions
were on the whole accurate enough to satisfy debate.

Medieval Ptolemaism was substantiated not only by visual
representations but by a vast literature based on the principle
of the spheres. The *Theorica planetarum* for example was a

popular thirteenth century textbook on Ptolemaic astronomy going through at least eight editions in northern Italy between 1472 to 1531. Georg Peurbach's influential *Theoricae novae planetarum* reinforced the Ptolemaic view, as did John of Sacrobosco's *Sphaera* mentioned earlier, a popular book which itself provoked a number of commentaries, even a short text from Galileo. The *Spera mundi*, a compilation of cosmological and geographical writings, published at Venice in 1478, includes Sacro Bosco's *Sphaera* as well as the theories of the twelfth century astronomer Gerardus Cremonensis. The *Spera mundi* – an almanac of philosophical musings, lists of the attributes of geographical regions and planetary data – represents the characteristic qualities of the type of cosmological treatise with which Camillo would presumably have been acquainted. However, as we shall see, he was probably also aware of some alternative theories on the matter.

Homocentrics

The homocentric astronomers believed that the earth was at the exact centre of the universe, around whose axis the rest of the cosmos span in concentric circles as opposed to the Ptolemaic system based on eccentric and epicyclic circles. The homocentric cosmology was based on a desire for order, proportion and symmetry.[11] However it seems that there was some debate as to exactly how many concentric spheres there were and the order in which the planets themselves were arranged.[12] Inspired by translations of Arabic authors such as Averroes, Thābit ibn Qurra and al-Battāni, Western philosophers such as Roger Bacon, Bernard of Verdun, Henry of Langenstein and Jean Buridan have all been associated with homocentric theories. Notable among later homocentrists were Giovanni Battista Amico and Girolamo Fracastoro. Amico suggested that the poles of the spheres had oscillatory movement. Fracastoro's *Homocentrica* published at Venice in 1538 was based on 'the principle that the axis of each [celestial] sphere should be perpendicular to the axes of the spheres immediately above and below it.'[13]

As mentioned in Chapter 2, Giulio Camillo was likely to have met Fracastoro at the Accademia Liviana, in Pordenone, around 1508. Despite this, however, Camillo's cosmology does not in fact bear much resemblance to the homocentrists'. First, while Camillo has an affinity with the idea of the unity and perfection of circularity, the motions that he ascribes to the planets are not themselves necessarily circular. Nor for that matter are they concentric or uniform. Camillo has two theories of planetary movement: one is based on the spiral; the other based on unpredictability, as I discuss. Second, Camillo's *L'Idea del Theatro* is perceived from the standpoint of the 'inner man' projecting his subjective earthly self onto the object of the heavens. This is necessarily done from the Earth's perspective, but does not mean that the earth is itself at the centre. But perhaps the greatest reason to dissociate Camilllo from the homocentrists is because Camillo's world picture is organic rather than uniform. He has more in common, in fact, with the 'fluid heaven' theory.

Fluid Heaven

The idea of a fluid through which the planets glide can be traced to the Stoics, who maintained that heaven was filled with *pneuma*, an animate fluid substance. Cicero's *De natura deorum* makes mention of the idea and it was revived by Camillo's hero Petrarch. Philosophers such as Pietro d'Abano, Robertus Anglicus and Andalo di Negro, advocated fluid heaven theories during the thirteenth and fourteenth centuries, while Giovanni Pontano promoted the idea well into the fifteenth century. By around the 1620s 'the debate over the fluidity of the heavens was very nearly concluded'.[14] However, it has been shown that supporters of the fluid heaven theory were widespread throughout Europe from London to Paris, Strasbourg to Padua.[15] Generically speaking, the fluid heaven hypothesis was that the planetary spheres were autonomous incandescent bodies that floated through the heavens 'like birds in the air, or fish in the sea'. The heavens themselves were filled with 'concentric zones of a fluid medium' creating 'a single vast fluid heaven.'[16]

Giovanni Pontano advocated a theory that the planets' movement was based on their own free will. Known primarily as a poet and statesman, Pontano's 'ornate astrotheology'[17] explicitly rejected a mathematical model to explain planetary movement. Writing exclusively in Latin, Pontano's epic poem, *Urania*, for example, composed in hexameters, tackled astronomical themes, while in his *De rebus coelestibus*, published in Venice in 1519, he focuses on the astrological aspects of cosmology. He brings a sense of order to his narrative through arranging his material in 'topics', with headings such as 'Fortitude', 'Liberality', 'Beneficence', 'Splendour', 'Obedience' and '*Conviventia*'.[18] The concept of the topics, Aristotelian in origin, certainly has echoes in the work of Camillo. As discussed in Chapter 4, *L'Idea del Theatro* itself is based on a topical, or encyclopedic, approach to the organization of felt experience and accrued knowledge.

More than Pontano, however, Camillo is close in spirit and thinking to the Paduan philosopher, Pietro d'Abano. Having studied medicine and philosophy at Paris, d'Abano became professor of medicine at Padua from 1306. D'Abano describes an animate world in which there is no division between the world of matter and the heavens. The material substance of the stars is as much a part of our bodies as our bones, affecting the very structure of our lives. There is a symbiotic connection between material and heavenly substance at an atomic level. In order to understand the stars, we need only to look at the workings of the body. Just as the currents of the blood flow through the arteries, so the stars move around the skies. He discusses the fluids of reproduction, of sperm, and menstrual flow affected by lunar phases, and projects the principle of regeneration onto the heavenly ether. Just as man and woman generate life, so the heavens reciprocate in a correspondent manifestation of time and being. For d'Abano, as spirit and matter are correspondent and interchangeable, so are astrology and astronomy. In his *Tractatus de venenis*, published at Mantua in 1473, he correlates astrology with medicine, providing a source of short treatises (or spells) that combine medicinal remedies with astrology and philosophy.[19] His *Conciliator differentiarum philosophorum et precipue medicorum Petri de Abano*, published in Mantua in 1472, is an impressive work in which he more fully expounds his philosophy. His quoted sources include Biblical scripture, Ptolemy, Boethius, Trismegistus, and others, many of which are familiar to Camillo. Like Camillo's *L'Idea del Theatro*, d'Abano's *Conciliator . . .* is a cosmic creation story which aims to synthesize all knowledge. He connects angelic beings to each of the planets in a strategic alignment of divine forces and heavenly spheres, reminiscent of Camillo's anthropomorphism of the planets on the first level of the Theatre.[20]

The intellectual climate was such that Camillo was likely aware of fluid heaven theories, though he does not specifically quote either Pontano or d'Abano in *L'Idea del Theatro*. However it is with another 'moisture-related' Renaissance astronomical theory that Camillo is expressly allied: celestial channels, or streams.

Celestial Streams

In his astronomical account, Christopher Clavius described the theory of celestial streams allegorically as the same as the system of veins within a body:

> . . . the whole heaven will be filled with channels in proportion to the multitude of stars, just like [the bodies of] animals, which are filled with many and various veins.[21]

It was also later described, disparagingly, by the Jesuit Nicola Partenio Giannettasio as a theory that propounded the idea that the planets 'run back and forth like rabbits' using 'celestial channels as tunnels'.[22] The adherents of this hypothesis were seemingly few in number and Clavius did not cite anyone by name. Nevertheless the fact that both he and Giannettasio, as late as 1688, discussed their work suggests that it was a significant strain of contemporary thought.

In *L'Idea del Theatro*, Camillo explicitly talks about the concept of 'supercelestial channels', 'celestial channels', and 'celestial streams'. He distinguishes between the 'supercelestial streams which do not wet' and the 'waters of this world, which do wet'.[23] The 'supercelestial streams' are from 'the waters above the Heavens'.[24] Elsewhere he discusses the 'moist heat'[25] of heaven, saying that it is 'liquid, fluid, agile, slippery and pleasing and sweet to the touch of nature'.[26] The waters above the firmament are a macrocosmic version of the earthly element of water that is manifested in streams, rivers and oceans. The 'supercelestial stream', though it characterizes similar qualities to water in its form, movement, density and 'germinative powers',[27] is dissimilar only in its essential quality of wetness.

For Camillo there is a vital equivalence between the body present in time and space and the eternal, between every particle of the body and the cosmos. This is operated through a correspondence on a sensual level with the 'inner man'. In the hair and beard and eyes, there is a tangible, personal, corporeal contact with the cosmic strength imparted through the 'celestial channels'. Bodily parts are connected to heavenly attributes. Elsewhere he says that just '. . . as the stars are the eyes of this world, so the plants and trees . . . [are] the skin and hair of its body and the metals and rocks are in the same way its bones . . .'.[28] And later, he says 'the world lives'. Vegetative matter, minerals, rocks, the cosmos and mankind all are in a state of constant reception of the celestial streams, the 'water of wholesome wisdom', reiterating his constant motif of an animate world in which every element is sentient of, and responsive to, its source.

Correspondent with the heavenly waters above the firmament, the celestial streams inseminate earthly matter not only with life but also with the 'spirit of life'. The 'streams', 'channels', and elsewhere what he calls the 'dew', of heaven is the vehicle by which this seminal heavenly influence is imparted.[29]

One of the images in the Theatre, 'The Young Girl with hair raised toward the Heavens', is based on the idea of celestial streams. She is meant to symbolise 'a vigorous thing either strong or trustworthy'. Camillo explains that the image is based on Plato's idea of man being a tree upside down 'since the tree has its roots below and man has his above'. He goes on, citing Origen and Jerome, to explain that the hair should be understood metaphorically as representing a part of the soul. In the same way, he suggests that all the parts of the body relate to an aspect of the 'interior man'. He says:

> **the tree draws to itself through its roots the nutritive moisture from the earth, so the beard and hair of our interior man should draw dew, that is, the living moisture from the influxes of the celestial channels, from whence comes all its strength.**[30]

The Young Girl with hair raised towards the Heavens . . . *vigorous . . . strong . . . trustworthy.*

For Camillo the spiritual or mystical aspect of creation is inseparable from the physical. His 'Young Girl' is, in every sense of the word, a vital expression of this philosophy with her electric mane alive with the 'spirit of life'.[31] The 'streams', 'channels', and elsewhere what he calls the 'dew', of heaven is the vehicle by which this seminal heavenly influence is imparted. He quotes from Canticles (Song of Solomon):[32]

> **. . . Thy head is like Carmel: and the hairs of thy head as the purple of the king bound in the channels . . .** Canticles 7:5

and makes a reference to the Psalms:

> **Behold how good it is, and how pleasant, where brethren dwell at one!**
>
> **It is as when the precious ointment upon the head runs down over the beard, the beard of Aaron, till it runs down the collar of his robe,**

It is a dew like that of Hermon, which comes down upon the mountains of Sion;

For there the Lord has pronounced his blessing, life forever.

Psalm 132(133)[33]

The 'channels', the 'ointment' and the 'dew' all represent for Camillo the celestial streams. Elsewhere he quotes from Luke: ' . . . The very hairs of your head shall be numbered . . . ' conveying the idea that the connections to the celestial streams of creation are apparent everywhere and in everything.[34]

Copernican Theory

Before looking at the innermost part of Camillo's Theatre, I would like to compare his work with Copernicus's *De Revolutionibus Orbium Coelestium*, first published in Nuremberg, in 1543. Camillo and Copernicus both worked or studied at the Universities of Padua and Bologna; though they did not necessarily meet, they shared a common intellectual parlance.[36] Of course, Camillo was not a mathematical astronomer. But he was not alone in this; it was common to value deductive reasoning over abstract mathematics as the preferred philosophical method of choice. Mathematics themselves were sometimes viewed if not with suspicion, then with a certain amount of scepticism. In fact, it was only in one branch of astronomy, judicial astrology, that the disciplines of mathematics and natural philosophy were combined.[37] It was Copernicus's mathematics which were unusual.

My focus is on the mutual intimacy of Copernicus's and Camillos' language to describe the world and heavens; their belief that the Earth moved; and on the consequences of the position of the Earth within the cosmos. The language and imagery of Copernicus's *De Revolutionibus* have been scrutinized in terms of classical, political as well as alchemical motifs.[38] Interpretations have varied: it was 'a natural philosophical justification';[39] it was an aesthetic that had its roots in Florentine Neoplatonism;[40] it was a 'magico-hermetic world-picture';[41] the preface was formulated using the rhetoric of persuasion;[42] it was a contemplative's response to the natural world revealed by God.[43] The reasons for Copernicus's reluctance to go public have been thoroughly questioned and scrutinized, *De Revolutionibus* only being published with the assistance of Rheticus in the year of Copernicus's death. Camillo's thesis was published posthumously. That it has survived at all is thanks to the efforts of his agent, Girolamo Muzio, in 1544. Had it not been for Muzio, *L'Idea del Theatro* would have remained hidden forever by 'dark veils'.[44]

The convoluted history of the publication of Copernicus's *De Revolutionibus* is worth re-telling, as it explains some of the dedicatory letters and preface to the work itself. Although it is uncertain at what point Copernicus began to write the book, the earliest observations in his work were made while he studied in Italy in around 1497 with the Bolognan Professor of Astronomy, Domenico Maria da Novara.[45] Copernicus's international reputation as an astronomer was established early, and he had given public lectures on astronomy in Rome in 1500.[46] For a number of years, after his return to Poland in 1505, colleagues and friends urged Copernicus to publish his theories, but he was reluctant. Eventually, it was not Copernicus but his disciple Rheticus who administered publication. An apocryphal tale has it that Copernicus was given a copy on his deathbed. Rheticus himself, however, did not see the task of publication through to the very end, and, famously, an anonymous announcement was inserted into the beginning of the book and published as though it was Copernicus's own words. The inserted passage stated that the calculations in *De Revolutionibus* were there 'not . . . in any way with the aim of persuading anyone that they are valid . . .' and urges the reader not to 'depart from this discipline [that is, astronomy] more foolish than he came to it.' The inserted passage also states that the hypothesis of the Sun being at the centre of the universe was no longer novel, in fact that it had been 'widely reported'.[47] The implication was that heliocentric ideas were common knowledge.

Copernicus himself begins *De Revolutionibus* with a dedicatory letter to Pope Paul III, in which he says:

> **I can well appreciate . . . that as soon as certain people realise that in these books . . . I attribute certain motions to the globe of the Earth, they will at once clamour for me to be hooted off the stage with such an opinion . . .[48]**

Then he explains that he set himself the task of 'reading again the books of all the philosophers' to find out whether anyone else had ever believed in the motions of the Earth. He says:

> **I hesitated for a long time whether to bring my treatise . . . into the light of day, or whether it would not be better to follow the example of the Pythagoreans and certain others, who used to pass on the mysteries of their philosophy merely to their relatives and friends, not in writing but by personal contact . . .[49]**

There are parallels, here, with the preamble to Camillo's *L'Idea del Theatro*, discussed in Chapter 5, and the belief that 'the oldest and wisest writers' protected 'the secrets of God', revealing them only to those who 'have ears to hear'.[50]

It may be that Copernicus included his prelude to the Pope merely to sweeten the pill of his hypothesis. But I do not think we can dismiss Copernicus's letter as a purely rhetorical device. Copernicus says that truths should only be imparted by word of mouth. This relates to a belief in the potent power of the word to effect transformative change, to the authority of *Ars Oratoria*. Camillo himself did not write down his hypothesis but instead dictated *L'Idea del Theatro* to Girolamo Muzio. Copernicus's and Camillo's hesitation at propounding their theories in public, in print, was rooted in a profound inhibition.

The *Tabular Catalogue of the Constellations and Stars* at the end of Book 2 of *De Revolutionibus* uses the language of bodily parts to describe star positions. This is due, in origin, to Ptolemy's naming of the constellations; nevertheless the intimacy with which the projected map of the heavenly bodies is described suggests a visceral response. 'On the right armpit', says Copernicus describing the position of a star in the constellation of *Hercules*; 'At the tip of the right foot'. 'On the beak' of *Cygnus*, or 'In the crook of the left wing'. 'On the shoulderblades' of *Andromeda*, or 'In the gaping mouth' of *Pegasus*. The list goes on for thirty-two pages in the same vein. The fascination for Camillo of the idea of the heavenly correspondence between the planets and our bodies is documented above.

Both Copernicus and Camillo ascribe motion to the Earth; however, their similarity ends there, as the *way* in which the Earth moves, for each man, is different. Copernicus explains 'triple motion', i.e. the revolution that creates night and day; the annual revolution around the sun; westwards motion.[51] Camillo, on the other hand, is much less specific. It is unclear from Camillo's hypothesis whether the movement that he describes is of the earth or the sun, as he ascribes the simile of giving birth to both.[52] Nevertheless, the fact of

The

earth

being

movable

is printed, in the manner above, in the margin of page 38 of the Florence (1550) edition of *L'Idea del Theatro*. There are a number of marginal annotations in the book that sum up the important points in the text, as well as astrological symbols to mark the relevant passages regarding the planets. It is unclear whether these were added by the printer, or by Muzio, or whether Camillo instructed them. But whatever their source, these annotations provide a précis of the most salient parts of Camillo's thesis. It is tempting to think that Camillo may well have developed these key themes orally; that the annotations provide clues to topics that Camillo would have unpacked fully in front of an audience. But in any case, while he is not explicit here about the manner of its movement, his belief in the motion of the earth at least places Camillo closer to Copernicus and at odds with the prevailing Ptolemaic orthodoxy, not to mention the homocentrist theorists many of whom state explicitly their belief in the stability of the planet.

Camillo's theory of celestial motion is closely allied to his conception of the 'spirit of Christ'. He says the 'spirit of Christ' moves over and through the world, being the source of generation, that this spirit is the binding principle of different elements:

> ... the truth of ... the birth of things, is that primary matter, being in every part ... things of a different nature such as water and earth ... finding themselves together ... would never be able to join together in a union, unless the spirit of Christ intervened, and entering into them, reconciled them to unfold the hidden seed ...

The movement of the 'spirit of Christ', which seems to originate in the region of the sun, reads like the description of a birth and a nuclear reaction:

> ... the spirit ... in everything, but hidden ... gasping, gives birth ... in the womb of nature, and thus joins it with motion. Thereafter joined by the eternal company with great love, it blows outside, impelling itself below to the dimension ... [It spreads] in a kind of circle ... And however much more it spreads, just so much more does it fuse and nearly send away with a new origin an almost continuous spirit spiralling from it ...[53]

Elsewhere, he reiterates the idea of planetary convulsions moved by love. Rather than a 'spiralling' or circular movement, as described above, however, Camillo here suggests unpredictable motion when he says that the Earth is 'shaken by many movements' because it is 'an impossible thing to give birth without movement'.[54] It is difficult, here, to ascertain whether Camillo is referring to terrestrial movements such as earth tremors, or quakes and landslides, or whether he is envisaging random movement on a planetary scale. In either case, his opinion about planetary movement places him closer to the 'fluid heaven' theorists, than to Copernicus in this instance. Copernicus discusses the irregularity of planetary movement evident in the precession and recession of the other planets to the Earth, but his solution to this is based on uniform circular orbits.

Copernicus illustrates his theory that the Earth revolves around the Sun, in a yearly orbit, in a diagram in Book One of *De Revolutionibus*. The diagram itself is similar in form to contemporary Aristotelian Ptolemaic pictures, with of course the crucial

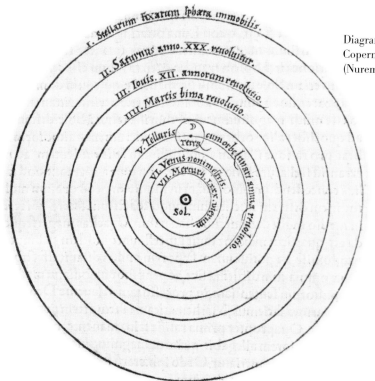

Diagram of the solar system from Copernicus's *De Revolutionibus* (Nuremerg, 1543).

difference that the sun rather than the earth is at the centre. In a
passage in which he quotes Trismegistus, Copernicus says:

> **In the middle of all is the seat of the Sun. For who in this most
> beautiful of temples would put this lamp in any other or better
> place than the one from which it can illuminate everything at the
> same time?**[55]

In *L'Idea del Theatro*, Camillo says that the Sun has 'the most
noble place of all the theatre'.[56] It is on the level of the Banquet
above the planets. But to discuss this fully, we must look at the
innermost levels of his Theatre.

Sun and Earth

Camillo describes the first level of the Theatre, where the planets
are positioned, beginning with the prevailing Ptolemaic order,
that is: the Moon; Mercury; and Venus. At the fourth place,
however, where the Sun would normally have been represented,
he places four distinct images. These are: the 'breadth of Being';
the fates; a tree and Pan. He then treats of the remaining planets
in the usual order, that is, Mars, Jupiter and Saturn. The Sun is
placed above the planets. He is explicit about its position: the
Sun is in the fourth place in the second level of the Theatre,
that is, at the level of the Banquet. Here, says Camillo, '. . . the
sun itself shall be discussed'.[57]

Camillo says that the 'breadth of Being' is represented by the
shape of a Pyramid, which symbolizes the 'Divinity, unrelated
and in relationship'; the appearance of the fates symbolize cause
and effect; the tree, or golden bough stands both for 'intelligible
things' as well as 'those we can only imagine . . . enlightened by
the active intellect'. Pan represents the three levels of the world.
Camillo says that in the representation of Pan:

> **. . . his head symbolizes the supercelestial [world], with his horns
> of gold which point upward, and with his beard, the celestial influ-
> ences, and with his starry hide, the celestial world, and with his
> goat legs, the inferior world.**[58]

The images of Pan, the tree, the fates and the Pyramid are placed in the position where, in the Ptolemaic order, it would have been usual to place the Sun. But the Sun is relocated to the level of the Banquet – the single planetary sphere to be so positioned. The Earth, on the other hand, is neither explicitly named nor placed by Camillo. Is this omission accidental? He goes to great lengths to explain that due to the magnificence and power of the sun it has been given its own noble location, and discusses the elemental, mythic and angelic attributes of each one of the other six planets. It seems unlikely that he would have forgotten to mention the Earth, in this context. As he states in the opening pages of *L'Idea del Theatro*, the very planets themselves are the original starting point for the whole Theatre, each of them resting on one of Solomon's Seven Pillars of Wisdom. The position of the Earth, however, never explicitly discussed in *L'Idea del Theatro*, is inferred. Though the Earth is not mentioned, could it be that we are to understand its glyph in the four images named above: Pan, the tree, the fates and the Pyramid? Each one of these images powerfully connects the mundane and spiritual, the planetary and heavenly.

It is significant that four images are represented at this point. The number four, according to medieval geometry, was associated with stability and, geometrically speaking, the four-cornered square was meant to represent the earth. The figure of Pan described by Camillo unites the three levels of the world: the supercelestial, the celestial and the inferior. With his goat legs resting on the inferior world, the body of Pan reaches up and connects all the other levels. This is a cosmically proportioned representation of Camillo's 'inner man', working at the level of the stars, yet positioned on the earth. Pan himself is described in terms of four elements: his head and golden horns symbolizing the supercelestial world, his beard, the celestial influences, or 'streams', his starry hide, the celestial world, and his goat legs, the inferior world.

Pyramid: *breadth of being.*

The Tree: *intelligible things.*

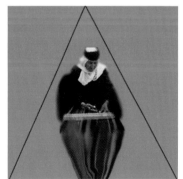

Fates: *cause and effect.*

Pan: *supercelestial.*

It is also interesting that the Fates should be positioned here. The Fates, according to Camillo, signify 'cause and effect'. The image indicates that: 'man is the cause of everything'.[59] At the beginning of *L'Idea del Theatro* Camillo says the Theatre is the place where first causes leading to their consequent effects will be discovered. From an astrological point of view, the Earth, and more precisely man on the Earth, is where the influence of the other planets will be experienced, the earth is the epicentre of astrological determinism. And yet if Camillo has altered the traditional positions of the Sun and the Earth and suggested that first causes come from the earth itself, what then?

In Camillo's model, causes and effects *stem from* the Earth, rather than the other way around. The relationship of the Earth to the other planets is active rather than passive. If this is the correct interpretation, Camillo's Theatre was a radical theory. As late as the seventeenth century, judicial astrology was still seriously considered, and yet Camillo was suggesting a new model based on autonomous self-sufficiency.

Chapter 7 Not the Whirlpool

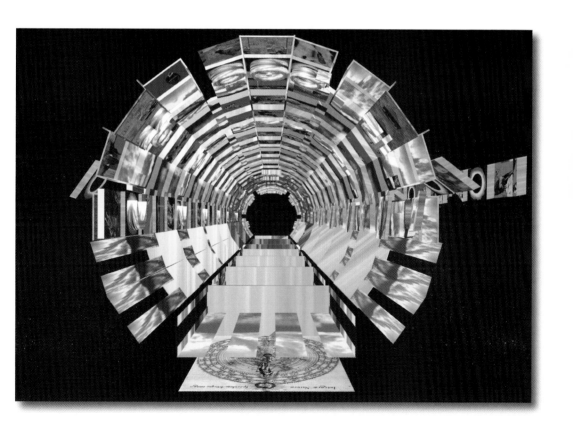

n astronaut is floating in space. There are no stars. But up ahead, there is a defined square of darkness, buoyant in the black. The astronaut floats towards the square, and then through it, to the other side.

The astronaut sees a burning sphere with white flames and then another sphere with a rising sun.

She moves towards the centre, piercing through deeper to the spheres below.

At last the astronaut passes through the final sphere to find a telescope of colour stretching into the distance. She looks down the length of the telescope: at the far end there is a little circle of darkness like the pupil of an eye. The astronaut is uncertain

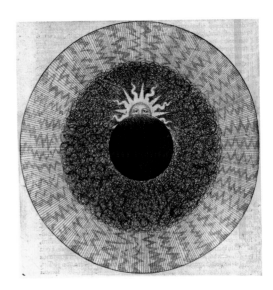

Robert Fludd, *Utriusque Cosmi.*

whether she's falling or rising. She catches a glimpse of the spheres above her through which she moved at first, to find they were never spheres at all but flat discs floating.

The interior of the telescope is filled with images. Some of the images are so familiar they feel as though they are part of her: her hometown, her childhood. They touch her like warm skin on a summer day or hot soup in winter. They fill her with longing. Other images are spicier and alien, exotic, challenging, alluring. When the astronaut reaches out, she can move into the centre of the pictures, and she finds that they are not images at all, but doorways. When she reaches out the doorways open to reveal new telescopes of infinity.

At last the astronaut returns through the tunnel of colour, through the discs of the spheres, to starless space.

The Virtual Reality model described above, was an important part of the research that led me to write and discover more about Giulio Camillo. The model itself was composed of hundreds of

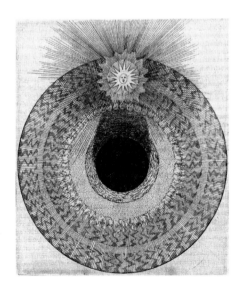

Wire frame of Virtual Reality model
of Camillo's Theatre, 2001.

computer-generated images.[1] The spheres, or discs, through which the astronaut moves at first, were taken from Robert Fludd's *Utriusque Cosmi* (Oppenheim, 1617).[2] These extraordinary drawings chart a creation story beginning in infinite darkness, which is subsequently illuminated by the light of God. The series is developed in a number of square format woodcuts, which contain a circular diagram that represents the universe, the Earth, God and atoms, all in one. The circular motif changes: at points it becomes like the churning bowels of the Earth – a kind of intestinal furnace of fire and smoke. At other times it is a dark centre, a horizon for the Sun. The images are across between symbols, emblems and illustrative working models of the universe.

I wanted to include Fludd's drawings in the model of Camillo's Theatre in order to make a visual connection between the eclectic creationism of the two authors, one from sixteenth-century Italy, the other from seventeenth-century Britain. In fact, serendipitously, I think that it highlighted something else. By moving through the centre of Fludd's black-and-white discs, to find the model of Camillo's Theatre stretching away into the distance, the viewer becomes aware that the essential ingredient in the Theatre is the position of the perceiver to the vanishing point, or infinity.

In this chapter I explore the centre of Camillo's Theatre – the position of the perceiver. As discussed in the previous chapter, Camillo's Theatre can be usefully appreciated within the context of astronomy. Camillo proposes a cosmological arrangement which shows that, in terms of planetary positioning, the Sun is pre-eminent; and that the Earth is on a similar plane to the Moon and the planets. However, this still leaves the question of the centre, of finding the optimum position from which the rest of the pantheon may be viewed.

An associate of Titian, Camillo was at the forefront of Italian ideas about pictorial space. Camillo's theories may themselves have had an effect on Serlio's new theories of stage design. As

I discuss, the calculus of Camillo's Theatre can, on one level, be assessed in terms of Serlio's ideas of the significance of the 'vanishing point' within a scenic setting. However, Camillo's ideas were rooted not only in perceptual analysis but also in philosophical theories. The origin of Camillo's *artificiosa rota*, for example, the whirlpool of artifice mentioned in Chapter 1, can be found in the philosophy of Nicolaus of Cusa. As I discuss, Cusa's ideas – his 'Learned ignorance' – are seminal to Camillo's Theatre.

Perspectival theory was well established by the time that Sebastiano Serlio discussed its use within the context of theatre design.[3] In Serlio's *Libro d'Architettura* (1545), he talks about the use of perspective in a stage setting, saying that it will enable the theatre practitioner to create a magnificent illusion. The crucial issue in creating this chimera is to find the place within the scene that relates to the 'vanishing point'. This, he says, 'is hard to demonstrate' and must change from scene to scene.[4]

With the introduction of the proscenium arch, each scene is given a frame. The vanishing point is worked out from the perspective of the members of the audience sitting in the auditorium. The theatrical setting created an illusion comparable to the illusion of depth that had been achieved in the art of painting, with the added advantage of it being alive. Serlio's actors would animate an optical illusion; inhabit a virtual world. I do not think that Camillo envisaged a *literal* Theatre space in the sense that Serlio did. Camillo's Theatre was a conceptual arena. Nevertheless, Serlio and Camillo bear comparison on the grounds of the levels of artifice to which they were prepared to go to recreate reality. In this endeavour they were co-discoverers. The 'Theatre', for both of them, was the place in which artifice would uncover truth.

If we apply the principle of perspective to the *images* in Camillo's Theatre, then, in effect, we will have as many vanishing points as there are pictures. As many views of infinity as images in the book. It is tantalizing to imagine how Titian would

Cross-section of a theatre in
Serlio's *Il Primo (Secondo) Libro
d'Architettura*, Paris, 1545.

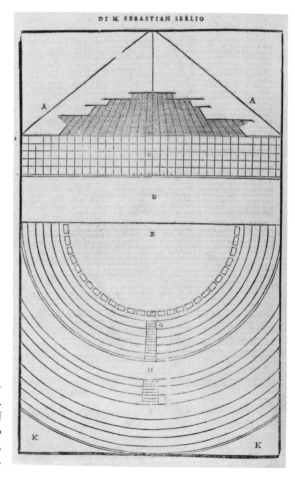

Serlio's ground plan of a theatre. The semicircular section relates to the auditorium.
The rectangular grid represents the front of
the stage, and the triangular area at the top
relates to the position of the vanishing point,
as seen from the auditorium.

Stage setting from Serlio's
Architettura (Paris, 1545).

The horizontal lines *ab* and *cd* show the front of the stage. The raked area begins at *cd.* Stage scenery, is painted with a base line extending along lines *xy*.

Serlio demonstrates how the stage and auditorium can be arranged in order to achieve the illusion of infinity from the audience's perspective. The stage must be slightly raked, he says, beginning at an area a metre or so from the front edge of the stage. The horizontal base lines for painted scenery can begin at the extreme right and left of the stage area, extending in a diagonal towards the back of the stage towards the vanishing point.

have dealt with this. I think Titian would have had a field day, encoding Camillo's information in complex images to be read on a number of planes. Camillo and Titian together would have created a whole illusionary world using the building blocks of language and imagery: a three-dimensional dream.

I imagine that Camillo was so familiar with the layout of the Theatre that he could move around it at will, in the same way that Viola describes the possibility of moving around a predetermined 'data space'. For me, in fact, Camillo is most alive when imagined as a performance, or conceptual artist. To hear him speak, giving one of his orations at the court of François 1ᵉʳ or the Pope or at the lodgings of Aldus Manutius, in Venice, would have been a rare act. Idea, image and text had equal valence for Camillo. They were part of the outer skin of man, his multicoloured coat. But Camillo, I think, had such a profound belief in the integrity of the 'inner man' that this outer skin of language and picture could be torn up, reassembled, collaged, broken and renewed without compromise.

To return to Camillo's whirlpool of artifice, the centre is where the reconciliation of opposites is made possible. In the *artificiosa rota* literary opposites are reconciled: 'arrival' becomes 'departure'. They are transformed, according to Camillo, at the centre, in the 'generative nucleus'. The National Library of Scotland has a copy of the original publication of *Delle Materie*, made in the year of Camillo's death in 1544. The *rota* is reproduced inside, the dead centre worn away from years of touching. In this *rota*, unlike in later editions, words are printed across the middle of the wheel. In language reminiscent of Nicolaus of Cusa, Camillo talks about moving from 'antecedents' to 'consequences', from 'opposites [to] all things contrary'. Then he asks a rhetorical question: 'what is the most beautiful and dignified thing we see in the sky?' Close to the centre of the wheel comes the answer: 'The Sun,' he says, 'without a doubt.'

Nicolaus of Cusa's *Docta ignorantia*, or 'Learned ignorance', was composed in 1440. Cusa is credited with being the first in the medieval period to have believed in the infinity of the universe.[5] He was also an early advocate of heliocentrism. Cusa's fifteenth-century doctrine of 'Learned ignorance' bears resemblance to the sixteenth-century's 'Serious Play', mentioned in Chapter 1. Both are views of the world that assert that the only thing we can be certain of is that we do not know anything, even if we pretend otherwise.

According to Cusa, God is infinite and the universe is interminate, by which he means that the universe is boundless.[6] Cusa reasons that *because* the universe is essentially non-definable, we can only hope to understand it by bypassing rationality altogether, and adopting the attitude of 'Learned ignorance'. Wherever the observer is positioned in the earth, 'he will believe himself to be in the centre,' says Cusa. Therefore the observer, on his own, will never achieve an accurate picture of the whole. In order to begin to appreciate the universe at large, distinct from one's own subjective point of view, one

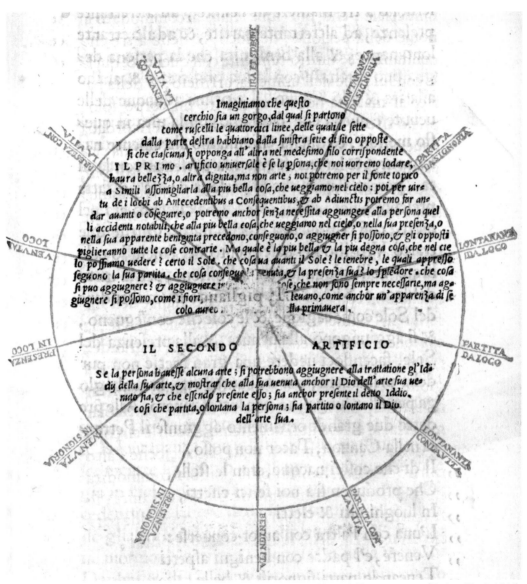

Artificiosa rota from Camillo's 'Due Trattati: L'uno delle materie . . . (Venice: Farri, 1544).

must combine 'diverse imaginations', that is, multiple pictures of the world, superimposing them together. This will allow the observer a fuller picture, but it will still not be complete. The observer must therefore practise learned ignorance. 'Learned ignorance' itself, is an ongoing outlook that aims to circumvent rational thought. Adopting this attitude, the viewer will begin to see that the world is 'Incorrigibly plural'.[7] 'It will appear almost as a wheel within a wheel, and a sphere within a sphere, having nowhere . . . either a centre or a circumference'.[8]

Cusa believed in the coincidence of opposites. All greatness and smallness, nearness and distance, the immediate and the remote, are united, for Cusa, within the 'infinite equality' of God. Opposites are reconciled and transformed into their contrary position. For Cusa, everything in the universe is relative, because only the absolute belongs to God. 'The absolute, infinite maximum does not, any more than the absolute, infinite minimum, belong to the series of the great and small. They are outside it, and therefore,' concludes Cusa, 'they coincide'. God is both at the centre of everything as well as at the edges: 'He is the centre of the earth and of all the spheres . . . He is at the same time the infinite circumference of all.'[9]

Just as Cusa believes in the coincidence of greatness and smallness, nearness and distance, Camillo imagines a system in which the 'material' of ideas is transformed into its contrary substance. In the *artificiosa rota*, Camillo was dealing with language. Inside the 'whirlpool of artifice', Camillo believed the opposites of the *rota* were reconciled. This was the no-man's land in the centre of the wheel where there was a space for unpredictability and change. In terms of the *rota* this change was specifically literary. Camillo intended that a similar operation was at work in his Theatre. It was a more complex system than the *rota* because it dealt not only with language, but imagery as well. The transformation, in terms of the Theatre, was a visual revolution.

In Camillo's conceptual Theatre, there is no stage. The images themselves are the vistas of action. Camillo is imagining a space that is, itself, potentially infinite. The signs in the Theatre, as well as being doorways to infinity, give clues for direction; they are route markers, to be mapped and followed, showing a way through the image-maze. Camillo, in effect, envisaged a kind of pictorial and linguistic calculus created of 'diverse imaginations'. His ideas were fed by a deep-rooted faith in the power of 'not-knowing'. The reason why, for Camillo, our learning must be ignorant, and our play is really serious, is because it is only by accepting the uncertainty, unpredictability, the randomness and capriciousness of the world that we can begin to come close to it. Things change inside the space of not-knowing. Cusa's learned ignorance helps to elucidate Camillo's serious play, just as there are similarities between Camillo's literary whirlpool of artifice and Serlio's visual vanishing point. One is formed of words and meaning, the other of images and infinity. For Camillo, meaning and infinity were fused.

Theoretically, the centre of the Theatre can be anywhere. But I think Camillo believed there is one unifying position from which the entire Theatre most truly is perceived. Wherever the observer is positioned in the earth, according to Cusa, 'he will believe himself to be in the centre.' But the deepest centre, the place from which – and to which – all the vanishing points of the images within the Theatre are directed, is the source. This is the place where 'diverse imaginations' are reconciled. This is the 'generative nucleus'. It is the centre of the whirlpool.

Epitaph

Giulio Camillo *c*.1480-1544

Eleven years after Camillo's death, an emblem was made in his memory.[1] It has a short Latin text by Achille Bocchi and a woodcut by the artist, Giulio Bonasone. The woodcut shows a nightingale on the branch of a tree looking into a pool of water. The nightingale is singing a song. On the other side of the pool stands a flock of river naiads, laughing at the little nightingale, because they see that he has been fooled by his own reflection in the water. Thinking that he is in the company of a rival, the nightingale sings louder and eventually dives into the pool to have it out with his supposed contender. But he finds that he is the only bird there, and emerges from the empty pool dripping in water. There is silence as he flies off into the blue.

The emblem can be read as an adaptation of the myth of Narcissus, who fell in love with his own reflection in a pool of water, while Echo, the nymph who loved him, watched from the sidelines. Where Narcissus sees, the nightingale hears. Where Echo, unseen, listens and repeats, the naiads listen and laugh in clear view. Narcissus sighs for love; the nightingale competes. This homage to Camillo is a strange, and ambivalent epitaph. The nightingale is challenging nothing but his own reflection yet his mighty, if pointless struggle produces music and laughter, which cannot be bad.

Maybe Bocchi intended that the naiads' laughter, in his emblem for Camillo, was to smack of ridicule. Or maybe he wanted us to remember that the naiads themselves *are* the water in which the nightingale sees his reflection. And as the essence, or Being, of the water itself, there must be an element of recognition in their mirth.

Endnotes

All reasonable efforts have been taken to obtain permission to reproduce material from sources. In hte event of a query, please contact the publishers.

Notes for Chapter 1

1. Camillo, Giulio, *L'Idea del Theatro* (Florence: Lorenzo Torrentino, 1550), pp. 10-11.
2. Altani, Federigo, 'Nuova Raccolta d'Opusculi Scientifici e Filologici' in *Memorie intorno alla vita* (Venice: Simone Occhi, 1755), pp. 239-88.
3. The 'Alethiometer' – the truth compass – of Philip Pullman's *His Dark Materials* trilogy is based on ideas of Camillo. For details on other artists see bibliography.
4. Yates, Frances, *The Art of Memory* (London: Pimlico, 1992), pp. 328-29. Originally published by Routledge & Kegan Paul, London, 1966.
5. Excerpt from SHAKESPEARE AND THE GODDESS OF COMPLETE BEING by Ted Hughes. Copyright © 1992 by Ted Hughes. Reprinted by permission of Farrar, Straus and Giroux, LLC. © The Ted Hughes Estate (London: Faber & Faber, 1992), pp. 32-3. Hughes says of 'Camillo's Memory Theatre', that it was one of 'the most peculiar memory systems to influence Bruno'. Though Hughes uses the terminology of 'Occult Neoplatonism', he shows some wariness.

    He says: 'Without assuming that Shakespeare was a devout Occult Neoplatonist, or was more than amused by the ingenuities, curious about the claims, and intri-gued by some of the concepts, one can suppose that out of this vast complex of archaic, magical, religious ideas and methods, the following items caught his attention:

    The idea of an inclusive system, a grand spiritual synthesis, reconciling Protestant and Catholic extremes in an integrated vision of union with the Divine Love.

    The idea of a syncretic mythology, in which all archaic mythological figures and events are available as a thesaurus of glyphs or token symbols – the personal language of the new metaphysical system…

    …The idea of these images as internally structured poetic images – the idea of the single image as a package of precisely folded, multiple meanings, consistent with the meanings of a unified system….' (pp. 32-3.)

    Hughes includes many other ideas in his list. I include only those that most closely relate to the theme of this work.
6. *The Theatre of Memory*, 31 March–5 May 2001, Collins Gallery, University of Strathclyde.
7. Ramachandran, V.S. & Blakeslee, Sandra, *Phantoms in the Brain* (London: Fourth Estate, 1988), p. 148. For other accessible and scholarly work on this subject, see Damasio, Antonio, *The Feeling of What Happens* (London: Vintage, 2000) and Greenfield, Susan, *Brain Story* (London: BBC

Worldwide, 2000). For an artistic perspective, the exhibition catalogue for Spectacular Bodies, 19 October 2000–14 January 2001, is recommended, Kemp, Martin & Wallace, Marina, Spectacular Bodies (London: Hayward Gallery Publishing, 2000).
8. Wenneker, Lu Beery, 'An Examination of L'Idea del Theatro of Giulio Camillo, including an annotated translation, with special attention to his influence on Emblem Literature and Iconography', (unpublished PhD Thesis: University of Pittsburgh, 1970). I have found Wenneker's translation very valuable; much of it appears in this work, for which I am grateful.
9. Imperial ambassador to Venice, 1539-46. Famous for his book collection, particularly of Greek manuscripts. He was assisted in acquiring this collection by a Dutch scholar, Arnoldo Arlenio. See Anthony Hobson, *Renaissance Book Collecting: Jean Grolier and Diego Hurtado de Mendoza, Their Books and Bindings* (Cambridge University Press, 1999).
10. Camillo, *L'Idea del Theatro*, dedicatory letter by Lodovico Domenichi, p. 4.
11. Quoted in Wenneker, 'An Examination of *L'Idea…*', p. 102.
12. Wylie, James A., *The History of Protestantism*, vol II, bk XIII, ch. XVIII, (London: Cassell, 1878), quoted at www. doctrine.org/history.
13. Yates, quoting *Enciclopedia italiana*, in *The Art of Memory*, p. 135.
14. Bolgar, R.R., *The Classical Heritage and its Beneficiaries*, (Cambridge University Press, 1954), p. 434.
15. Levi, A.H.T., ed., Collected Works of Erasmus, vol 28, *Ciceronianus*, trans. Betty Knott-Sharpe, (University of Toronto Press, 1986), pp. 562- 3, n.308.
16. Camillo, Giulio Delminio, De L'Imitation, trans. into French by Françoise Graziani with introduction and notes by Lina Bolzoni, (Paris: Les Belles Lettres, 1996). Author's translation.
17. Yates, *The Art of Memory*, p. 137.
18. It was a commonplace of the time to believe that mysteries could be revealed through the numerological analysis of text. Marsilio Ficino had written that 'The old custom of the philosophers was to conceal the divine mysteries with the numbers and figures of mathematics and with poetic fictions'. Ficino, Marsilio *Omnia Opere Plotini*, vol. 1, ed. Frederick Creuzer (Oxford University Press, 1835), p. xi. Camillo says '…the Lord's Prayer, according to the Hebrew text written by Matthew, is of forty nine words.' Camillo, *L'Idea del Theatro*, p. 13.
19. See Carruthers, Mary, *The Book of Memory* (Cambridge University Press, 1990), pp. 251-3. Carruthers suggests that the origin of the wheels is in 'the practical discipline of monastic prayer'; see also Bolzoni, Lina, trans. Jeremy Parzen, The Gallery of Memory: Literary and Iconographic

Models in the Age of the Printing Press, (University of Toronto Press, 2001), pp. 23-82 and Yates, pp. 178-196.

20 The sonnet was in celebration of Ercole d'Este, when he became Duke of Ferrara. See Bolzoni, *The Gallery of Memory*, pp. 43-4.

21 Ibid., p. 43.

Notes for Chapter 2

1 Double portrait with Agostino Beazzano, painted around 1516. Oil on canvas; Galleria Doria Pamphilj, Rome.

2 Camillo is known to have lectured at Serlio's house. There is another connection through Citolini, one of his students, who was named as a witness in Serlio's Will. Citolini was later to use Camillo's work as his own. See ch. 4.

3 For a contemporary edition of Camillo's work, see Camillo Delminio, Giulio, ed. Lina Bolzoni, *L'idea del teatro e altri scritti di retorica*, (Turin: Edizioni RES, 1990).

4 Camillo, *L'Idea del Theatro*, p. 39.

5 See Wenneker, 'An Examination of *L' Idea…*', p. 377 [p. 39] n.2.

6 Camillo Delminio, Giulio, *Due Trattati … l'uno delle Materie, che possono uenir sotto lo stile dell'eloquente: l'altro della Imitatione*, (Venice: Nella stamperia de Farri, 1544).

7 Camillo, *L'Idea del Theatro*, p14.

8 Nicolaus of Cusa described it as that which 'has no name', it is 'Possibility or Being-able-to-develop or Underlying', quoted in Roob, Alexander, *Alchemy and Mysticism*, (Taschen, 1997), p. 175.

9 Altani, *Memorie intorno…*, pp. 244-5. Author's translation.

10 On Ficino's *De Amore*, for example, Levi has said its 'prodigious 'influence' … has often been catalogued, but it was too diffuse and all-permeating for any list' (p. 124), while the 'eclectic' Pico, who 'inspired Erasmus…combined a belief in magic and astrology with a belief in human liberty not dissimilar to Ficino's' (p. 127). Levi, Anthony, *Renaissance and Reformation*, (Yale University Press, 2002).

11 Camillo's named sources, in order of appearance in *L'Idea del Theatro*, are as follows: Biblical scripture, (specifically, Matthew, Mark, Luke, John, Exodus, Apocalypse, Esdras, the Psalms, Numbers, Ezechiel, Proverbs, Isaiah, Hebrews, Romans, Galatians, Colossians, Acts, Thessalonians, Wisdom, Genesis, Canticles, Philippians).

Others (numbers in brackets refer to page numbers): Malissus (7), Hermes Trismegistus (8, 10, 18, 20, 21, 38, 46, 51, 53), Ammonius Saccas (9), Vergil (10, 16, 32, 36, 49, 52, 52, 58, 61, 67, 74, 82), Maximus Tyrius (12), Cicero (12, 40, 59, 84), Aristotle (12, 18, 32, 58, 59, 83), Homer (17, 27, 29, 31, 40, 49), Plato (17, 21, 29, 41, 54, 57, 70, 79), Ramon Lull (18), Plotinus (19, 22, 23, 24, 58), Petrarch (19, 49, 65, 66, 74, 75) 'Pythagoreans' (18, 20, 21, 22), 'Platonists' (20, 26, 37, 50, 62, 67), Morienus (22), St. Augustine(24)

'Peripatetics' (25, 33), Gregory Nazianzus (30), Pliny (39, 45), Iamblichus (39), Lucretius (39), Origen (41, 55), Jerome (41, 55), Macrobius (46), Euripedes (52), Rabbi Simeon (53), St. Thomas (59), Simplicius (60), Landino (83), Boccaccio (84), Anaxagoras (31).

12 Camillo, *L'Idea del Theatro*, p. 39. The reference is to *De Rerum Natura*, 4. 710-35. Camillo also mentions Lucretius in *Trattato Dell' Imitation*. Koyré says that the first reference to Lucretian cosmology was by Giordano Bruno. In fact, Camillo is earlier. See, Koyré, Alexander, *From the Closed World to the Infinite Universe*, (Baltimore: Johns Hopkins Press, 1957), p. 6.

13 There had been a significant Jewish minority in Venice from the tenth century, while the first Jewish ghetto in Europe had been established in Venice around 1516.

14 See Bolzoni, *Gallery of Memory*, p. 81.

15 The upper triad is formed by *Kether*, will, *Cochma*, wisdom, and *Bina*, intelligence. Below this, *Chessed*, love, mercy and goodness, is balanced by *Gebura*, severity and punitive power. *Gebura* and *Chessed* are harmonised through *Tiphereth*, generosity, splendour and beauty. From these, flow *Nezach*, endurance, victory, *Hod*, magnificence and majesty and *Jesod*, the ground of all procreative powers. From all of these is made manifest *Shekhinah*, the kingdom, the dwelling of God in creation. The relationships between each of the Sfirot are subtle and dynamic and to be understood in terms of movement, with each matrix affecting the others. There are countless other variations of the tree and there are many levels on which the tree can be understood.

16 Camillo, *L'Idea del Theatro*, p. 36.

17 *Ibid.*, p. 63.

18 *Ibid.*, p. 73

19 The idea of a banquet in which transformation takes place had a rich currency and though Dante's *Convivium* was important in this instance to Camillo, there may be other influences. Ficino's *In Platonis Convivium* was available from 1469. The central rite of the Mass uses the motif of the Last Supper.

20 Camillo, *L' Idea del Theatro*, p. 17.

21 *Ibid.*, p. 20.

22 *Ibid.*, p. 21.

23 *Ibid.*, p. 25.

24 *Ibid.*, p. 29.

25 *Ibid.*, p. 30.

26 *Ibid.*, p. 54.

27 *Ibid.*, p. 55. He adds that Christ's body was made of this 'virginal earth and of the most pure blood of the Virgin Mary'.

28 *Ibid.*, p. 57.

29 *Ibid.*, p. 60.

30 *Ibid.*, p. 62.

[31] Psalm 104: v. 4.

[32] Camillo, *L'Idea del Theatro*, p. 67.

[33] *Ibid.*, p. 79.

[34] *Ibid.*, pp. 79- 86.

[35] While *L' Idea del Theatro* is divided into seven sections, each section itself divided again by seven further divisions, the number of descriptions of imagery at each level in Camillo's plan is uneven. Every section of the Theatre contains descriptions of images – but the number of images for each section varies. No section contains more than seven images, but some can contain as few as one image.

[36] Bolzoni, *Gallery of Memory*, pp. 12 & 23-82.

[37] Viola, Bill, *Reasons for Knocking at an Empty House*, (MIT Press in association with Anthony d'Offay Gallery, London, 1995), p. 108.

[38] Eliade, Mircea, trans. Willard R. Trask, *The Myth of The Eternal Return*, (London: Arkana, 1989), pp. 17- 18.

Notes for Chapter 3

[1] There were 4151.

[2] An alternative date given for his birth is 1466.

[3] The character of Nosoponus, for example, is said by some to be based on Christophe de Longueil, a Northerner, while others think he is to be based on the Italian Cardinal Bembo. See *Opus Epistolarum Des. Erasmi Roterdami*, ed. H.M. Allen, (Oxford: Oxford University Press, 1937), *Ep:* 2632,n.196. References to the Epistles herein afterwards referred to as Allen *Ep.*

[4] Levi says that the speech described was probably given on The Day of the Parasceve, or Good Friday, 6 April 1509, in the presence of Pope Julius II. See the introduction and notes and p. 562 n.306, in Erasmus, ed. A.H.T. Levi, *Collected Works of Erasmus 28, Ciceronianus* (University of Toronto Press: 1986). See also Bolzoni, Lina, 'Erasmo e Camillo: il dibattitio sul'imitazione'. *Filologia antica e moderna* 4 (1993), p. 73; Chomarat, Jacques, *Grammaire et Rhetorique Chez Erasme*, vol 2, (Les Belles Lettres, Paris, 1981), pp. 939 & 1090.

[5] Quoted in Sandys, J.E., *Harvard Lectures on the Revival of Learning* (Cambridge University Press, 1905), p. 159.

[6] Levi, *Ciceronianus*, p. 324.

[7] Erasmus, *Ciceronianus*, p. 342.

[8] *Ibid*, p. 352.

[9] *Ibid.* p. 389.

[10] *Ibid.*, pp. 397- 9.

[11] *Ibid.*, p. 394. A year before the publication of the *Ciceronianus*, Erasmus had written to Francisco Vergara, professor at the University of Alcala, explicitly equating Ciceronianism with paganism. See Allen *Ep.* 1885, VII. 193-4, 11 and Halkin, Léon-E., *Erasmus* (Oxford: Blackwell, 1994), pp. 217-18.

[12] An example can be seen in the treatment of Guillaume Budé, the great scholar of the French court, secretary to Francis 1 and instigator of the Bibliothèque Nationale. Erasmus and Budé's relationship had begun around 1516 and their correspondence over a decade shows a true engagement and meeting of minds. The apogée of Erasmus's professed respect for Budé can be seen in a letter to Étienne Poncher, Bishop of Paris, in 1517, in which he calls him 'most certainly the glory of France'. However, in *Ciceronianus*, Budé is cited as being inferior to the printer Josse Bade as a failed Ciceronian, closely followed by a disparaged Jacques Lefèvre. This of course could be taken as a compliment, as there is no great accolade in being praised by Nosoponus, however Budé did not take it that way. A flurry of letters was written to Erasmus asking him to rethink his appraisal, but in the end it contributed to the rupture of Budé's and Erasmus's relationship.

[13] See Scaliger, Jules-Cesar, *Orationes Duae Contra Erasmum, Oratio Pro. M. Tullio Cicerone Contra Des. Erasmum (1531) & Adversus Des. Erasmi Roterod. Dialogum Ciceronianum Oratio Secunda (1537)* Ed. Michel Magnien, (Geneva: Droz, 1999), p. 11. Scaliger followed up his initial attack six years later with *Adversus Des. Erasmi Roterod. Dialogum Ciceronianum Oratio Secunda* (Paris, 1537), another derisory tract. Étienne Dolet's furious *Erasmianus* was published in 1535 and there were also works from Ortensio Lando and Gaudenzio Merula among others. For a survey of responses, see Pigman III, G.W. 'Imitation and the Renaissance Sense of the past: the reception of Erasmus' *Ciceronianus*' in *Journal for Medieval and Renaissance Studies*, 1979 (9): 155-77.

[14] *Ciceronianus*, p. 384.

[15] *Ibid.*, p. 386.

[16] Allen *Ep.* 1347: 263- 71. Translation in Levi, *Collected Works*, vol. 9, p. 421.

[17] Allen *Ep* 1347: 263- 5

[18] It was first published in answer to a pamphlet that had been circulated by the poet, Peter Cursius. In the pamphlet Cursius had defended the innumerable Italian men whose talents he thought bore comparison with those of Erasmus; among them he named Giulio Camillo. Allen *Ep* 3007, n.54.

[19] Cum Petro Phaedra, cuius eloquentiam tum Roma pro Cicerone mirabatur, mihi fuit propinqua familiaritas, cum Iulio Camillo me nonnunquam eadem iunxit culcitra. Allen, *Ep* 3032: 219- 22.

[20] See Allen *Ep.* : 2632: 174- 97 and 2657: 30-60.

[21] Not the least of the incongruities is that at the time Zwichem said he saw Camillo in Venice, Camillo was in fact in Bologna laid up with a bad knee! See Wenneker, 'An Examination of *L' Idea…*', p. 19.

[22] Allen *Ep*:2682:8-13: 'Amphiteatrum nae tu scite depinxisti, opus profecto tali Rege dignum. Nunc haud admiror si

quosdam male habuit meus Ciceronianus. Hinc videlicet, hinc illae lacrymae. Equidem illis istam gloriam non inuideo, sed vereor ne molitores isti non leuiorem trageoediam excitent in studiis quam Lutherus excitauit in religione.'

23 This and the following quotations are from F. Robinson's English translation of *Trattato dell' Imitazione*. See Robinson, K., 'A Search for the Source of the Whirlpool of Artifice' (Glasgow University PhD thesis: 2002), pp 182-205. I am very grateful to my father for this translation and for his fiendish insights into Camillo and Erasmus.

24 While the speech in question was in 1509, *Ciceronianus* wasn't published until 1528, and Fedra had died in 1516.

25 Ludovico Dolce and the Marchese del Vasto were important, as well as Gilbertus Cognatus Erasmus's secretary; his reiteration of the letter from Zwichem kept the memory of the Theatre alive long after Camillo was dead. See above.

26 For an interesting discussion of this issue see: De Luca, Elena, 'Silent Meanings: Emblems, Lay Culture and Political Awareness in Sixteenth-Century Bologna' *Emblematica*, 12 (2002), 61-81.

27 Valla, Lorenzo, *On the True Good*, quoted in Seigel, Jerrold E. *Rhetoric and philosophy in Renaissance humanism: the union of eloquence and wisdom, Petrarch to Valla* (Princeton: Princeton University Press, 1968), p. 139.

28 Letter to Johann von Botzheim, Basel, 30 January 1523, Allen *Ep.* 1341A: 137- 8.

29 Barker, William, *The Adages of Erasmus* (University of Toronto Press, 2001), p. xxviii.

30 Or twenty-two, depending on his birth date.

31 It was finally published by Froben in May 1520.

32 Erasmus, ed. Craig R. Thompson, *Collected Works of Erasmus Vol. 23: Antibarbari/Parabolae* (Toronto: University of Toronto Press, 1978), p. 58.

33 Painted c.1508-10. See Baring, Anne & Cashford, Jules, *The Myth of the Goddess: Evolution of an Image* (London: Arkana, 1991), p. 593.

34 The origin of the horns is biblical, possibly arising from the equivalence, in Hebrew, of the words 'horned' and 'radiated'; see Walker, Barbara G., *The Woman's Encyclopedia of Myths and Secrets* (San Francisco: Harper & Row, 1983), p. 410.

35 Allen *Ep* 2533:109-13; cf *Ep* 393:18-28, Quoted in *Antibarbari/Parabolae*, p. xxiii.

Notes for Chapter 4

1 Born around 1433, Colonna was ordained in 1465. He was incorporated at the University of Padua in 1473. Other theories have suggested that Colonna was a Roman Prince, the great-nephew of Cardinal Prospero Colonna. This Prince was divested of all wealth and privileges on charges of heresy, and became a Dominican monk for the remainder of his life. See Colonna, Francesco *Hypnerotomachia Poliphili*, trans. Joscelyn Godwin (London: Thames & Hudson, 1999), pp. xiii-xiv.

2 Colonna, *Hypnerotomachia*, p. 11.

3 This is the Hercynian Forest. In the Forest, says Poliphilo, the trees 'would not allow the sun's welcome rays to reach the damp soil, but covered it like a vaulted roof with dense leaves that the nurturing light could not penetrate' (*Hypnerotomachia*, p. 13). There 'was nothing but the lairs of dangerous beasts and caverns full of noxious creatures and fierce monsters' (p. 14). Here we find the first correlation with Camillo, who, early in *L'Idea del Theatro*, uses the metaphor of a wood to describe the Inferior, Celestial and Supercelestial worlds. He says:

> If we were in a great wood and wished to see the whole of it well, staying in it, we would be unable to satisfy our wish, since we would be able to see only a small part of the view about us, the trees around blocking for us the view of things far off. (*L'Idea del Theatro*, pp. 11-12).

We must find an incline, says Camillo, and rise to the top of a hill in order to recognize the shape of the landscape.

4 All of whom, apart from Leda, are mentioned in Camillo's Theatre.

5 Colonna, *Hypnerotomachia*, p. 224.

6 *Ibid.*, p. 326.

7 *Ibid.*, p. 358.

8 *Ibid.*, p. ix.

9 Yates, *The Art of Memory*, p. 130. Schama, Simon, *Landscape and Memory*, (London: Fontana Press, 1995), p. 272.

10 See Jung, Carl, *Psychology and Alchemy*, trans., R.F.C. Hull, (London: Routledge Kegan Paul, 1980) p. 86.

11 Colonna, *Hypnerotomachia*, p. xii.

12 *Ibid.*, p. 41

13 Ancient text examples: pp. 169 & 213. Pictures of action examples: pp. 18 & 76. Architectural monuments examples: pp. 26 & 129.

14 E.g. the 'wolf, lion and dog' emblem in the picture of the procession, as discussed below.

15 I cannot do Colonna's work justice in these two short chapters, but hope that I shall contribute some statement specifically as regards Camillo's *L'Idea del Theatro*.

16 Camillo, *L'Idea del Theatro*, p. 26.

17 *Ibid.*, p. 17.

18 *Ibid.*, p. 79.

19 *Ibid.*, p. 26.

20 Horapollo *The Hieroglyphics*, trans. Alexander Turner Cory (London: William Pickering, 1840) Bk 3, LXXXIV, pp. 137-8.

21 It is interesting that a publication in England, of 1596, in which the writings of 'divers Latine Authors' were (anonymously) represented also makes use of the image of

the elephant. In Thomas Johnson's *Cornucopia, or Diverse Secrets: Wherein is contained the rare secrets in Man, Beasts, Foules, Fishes, Trees, Plantes, stones and such like…* (London: William Barley), the author says: 'The Elephant though never so outrage[d], yet seeing a Ram is often tamed'. Amongst many other animals, he talks about lions and wolves, which form a part of the next image shared by Colonna and Camillo. Johnson says:

> The Lion is thought to be tamed by none other means than with burned firebrands, which he utterly detesteth and is a feared of: the Wolf, who feareth neither staff nor iron, yet the casting of a stone is so contrary to him, that in the same place where he is hit with a stone are worms engendered.

Johnson, Thomas, *Cornucopiae…* (London: William Barley, 1596), no page numbers. Johnson's short work is unillustrated, like Camillo's, but the text-images that he describes have their roots in earlier work such as Horapollo's, which used the visual sign as the message-medium.

22 Eliade, *The Myth of The Eternal Return*, p. 35.
23 See Eliade, pp. 87-92.
24 *Ibid.*, p. 39.
25 *Ibid.*, pp. 44- 6.
26 *Ibid.*, p. 145.
27 *Ibid.* p. 54.
28 *Hypnerotomachia*, p. 326.
29 *Ibid*, p. 344.
30 Petrarch, *Africa*, III, 156.
31 Camillo, *L'Idea del Theatro*, p. 46.
32 Regarding the Moon as a measure of cyclical time, see Eliade, pp. 86-8.
33 Camillo, *L'Idea del Theatro*, p. 51.
34 Relational activities themselves of course might be said to be almost all human activities.
35 *Hypnerotomachia*, p. 346.
36 See Carruthers, p. 72.
37 See Carruthers, pp. 4-5 for an account of Thomas's own extraordinary use of memory.
38 Minds maps and memory aides are big business. Contemporary memory books include Tony Buzan's *Use Your Memory*, (London: BBC Books, 1996), *The Amazing Memory Book* (London: Duncan Laird Publishers, 2001), by Dominic O' Brien and *The Great Memory Book*, (USA: The Brain Store, Inc., 1999) by Karen Markowitz & Eric Jensen.
39 *Rhetorica Ad Herennium*, III, xxii, quoted in Yates, *The Art of Memory*, pp. 25-6.
40 Carruthers, p. 122.
41 *Ibid.*, p. 34.
42 See Green-Pederson, Niels Jørgen, *The Tradition of the Topics in the Middle Ages*, (Munich: Philosophia Verlag, 1984), pp. 15 –20.

43 In discussing *topoi*, Yates quotes from Aristotle's *Topics*:
> For…a person with a trained memory, a memory of things themselves is immediately caused by the mere mention of their places (Τόποι) . . . these habits . . . will make a man readier in reasoning, because he has the premises classified before his mind's eye, each under its number. *Topica*, 163^b 24-30 (Quoted in *The Art of Memory*, p. 46.)

Yates interprets the passage as follows:
> There can be no doubt that these *topoi* used by persons with a trained memory must be mnemonic *loci*, and it is indeed probable that the very word 'topics' as used in dialectics arose through the place of mnemonics. Topics are the 'things' or subject matter of dialectic which came to be known as *topoi* through the places in which they were stored. (*The Art of Memory*, p. 46.)

Yates's conflation of the dialectical *topoi* with mnemonic *loci* confuses the end, and the means to the end. While mnemonic techniques (whether or not these involved the adoption of *loci*) may have been essential during the era before the advent of print in remembering the ingredients of a dialectical argument or proposition, the mnemonics themselves were only tools. Granted, they were important tools – but they were not 'universals'. The 'universals' (despite the slipperiness in defining them) were the outcomes of a reasoned dialectic; or were at least the dialectical 'givens', or stages, within an argument leading to an outcome (or if not an outcome, then at least a further 'given', or *topos*). That these may sometimes have been brought (internally) to the mind of a thinker by the means of graphic imagery does not make the image itself the *topos*. In other words, in terms of a medieval dialectical proposition posited in terms of an internal set of mnemonic imagery, the medium shouldn't be confused with the message!

44 Carruthers, Mary, *The Craft of Thought* (Cambridge University Press, 1998), p. 3.
45 MacGregor, Neil, with Erika Langmuir, *Seeing Salvation* (London: BBC Worldwide, 2000), p. 153.
46 MacGregor differentiates Fra Angelico's images at San Marco from 'the images of the classical art of memory', saying 'they are not "mental" but actually exist as paintings; and they are not, as in antiquity, invented by the person using them, but part of a wide and pre-established tradition' (p. 157). I agree that there are differences between Fra Angelico's images and, for example, hieroglyphic/mnemonic systems such as those developed by Romberch but I would not choose the same reasons as MacGregor.
47 MacGregor, p. 160.
48 Wenneker, pp. 403-5.
49 In the first commentary there are identical or very similar passages in the emblems represented by *Prometheus, The Struggle of Reason and Appetite, Argus, the Model or Frame-*

work of the World, Endymion or the Death of the Holy Men, Human Appetite, Mercury offering Diana a Garment, and *Gorgons, or the Three Souls of Man.* In the second commentary, there are similarities in the description of Cerberus, and the images to represent the signs of Cancer and Capricorn. For more on all this, see Wenneker, pp. 117-39.

50 See Achille Bocchi's *Symbolicae quaestiones* (Bologna: Nuova Accademia Bocciana, 1555), Book 5, Emblem CXLVII.The hieroglyphs are slightly re-arranged in order to fit on the scroll held out by the angel in the picture, nevertheless, each element of the hieroglyphic scheme is faithfully represented, suggesting that the hieroglyphs are not regarded as decorative but as a systematic language.

51 *Ibid,* Book 1, Emblem I; Book II, Emblems XXXVI and XLIX.

52 *Ibid.,* Book I, Emblem XXII; Book IIII, Emblem CXV; Book V, Emblem CXXXIII. There are other processional triumphs represented in *Symbolicae quaestiones,* e.g. Book II, Emblems XLII and XLIIII, however these do not follow as closely to the pattern of the *Hypnerotomachia,* i.e. frontally positioned centurion's armour, with crossed spears, swords or shields creating strong diagonals below, above and/or behind the armour.

53 *Ibid.,* Book II, Emblem XLVIII; Book IIII, Emblem XCVII. Obelisks appear several times in the *Hypnerotomachia* both with, and without, circular orbs at the apex, or text/hieroglyphs on or near the base.

54 Watson discusses the difficulties in identifying the artist of the Bocchi emblems; see Watson, Elisabeth See, *Achille Bocchi and the Emblem Book as Symbolic Form* (Cambridge: Cambridge University Press, 1993) p. 67. For a biography of Bonasone, see Cirillo, Madeleine, B., 'Giulio Bonasone and Sixeenth-Century Printmaking' (unpublished PhD. Thesis: University of Wisconsin, 1978). For an overview of Bonasone in relation to Italian printmaking of the period, see *The Print in Italy 1550-1620* (Edinburgh: National Galleries of Scotland, 2003), catalogue to exhibition at National Gallery, Edinburgh.

55 De Luca, Elena, 'Silent Meanings: Emblems, Lay Culture and Political Awareness in Sixteenth-Century Bologna' *Emblematica,* 12 (2002), 61-81.

Notes for Chapter 5

1 Dante, trans. Mark Musa, *Paradise* (Penguin Classics, 1986), 29:139-40.
2 Camillo, *L'Idea del Theatro,* p. 7.
3 Dante, *Paradise,* 29: 76-82.
4 Carruthers, Mary, *The Book of Memory,* (Cambridge University Press, 1990), p. 57.
5 *Ibid.,* p. 55.
6 Camillo, *L'Idea del Theatro,* pp. 47-8.
7 In talking about this image, there is an immediacy about

Camillo's prose that suggests that he is describing in detail a picture that he is seeing in his mind's eye – you get the impression that this image, in particular, must have existed as a tangible object.

8 Colonna, *Hynerotomachia,* p. 325.
9 *Ibid.,* p. 95.
10 *Ibid.,* p. 96.
11 This is not a Neoplatonic memory of universals already 'imprinted in the soul'. See Carruthers, *The Book of Memory,* p. 56.
12 Colonna, *Hypnerotomachia,* p. 122.
13 Incidentally, if Colonna's map of Cytherea, is viewed not as a flat ground plan – not as spokes radiating from a wheel – but as an illusion of infinite depth, it literally takes on another dimension. Poliphilo's journey inward, to where the Theatre is, at the very centre of the island, has brought him, in a sense, to the vanishing point.
14 Colonna, *Hypnerotomachia,* p. xvi.
15 *Ibid.,* p. xvi.
16 Wenneker suggests that this may refer to a discussion in the *Epinomis* about the 'relative unimportance of geographic location…of the hereafter compared to the rewards to be found in it'. See Wenneker, p. 373, n.26.
17 Camillo, *L'Idea del Theatro,* p. 26. The description of Venus, here, is at the level of the Banquet. For a fuller explanation see Ch. 2.
18 Colonna, *Hypnerotomachia,* pp. 324-5.
19 *Ibid.,* p. 346. It is here that the image of the wolf, lion and dog, discussed in the previous chapter is displayed.
20 *Ibid.,* p. 347.
21 *Ibid,* p. 352.
22 *Ibid.,* p. xiii.
23 There are CXLVII Epigrams.
24 The long discussion about the use of the Latin language, with copious references to Cicero, that forms a part of the book also makes me wonder whether this may have been one of the works that gave rise to Erasmus's charge of 'Ciceronianism'.
25 Serlio, Sebastiano, trans., Allardyce Nicoll, *The Second Book of Architecture (Il Primo (Secondo) Libro d'Architettura),* Paris, 1545, in Hewitt, Barnard ed., *The Renaissance Stage, Documents of Serlio, Sabbattini, and Furttenbach,* (University of Miami Press, 1958), pp. 63-74.
26 The academician, Bernadino Partenio (c. 1500-89), remembered hearing Camillo lecture at Serlio's house in Venice, when he was a boy, and compared his eloquence and erudition to a god. See Bolzoni, *The Gallery of Memory,* p. 31.
27 See Robinson, 'A Search for the Source…', p. 204.
28 The Garden was planned by the Venetian, Daniele Barbaro, drawing on suggestions from the medieval *Horti Conclusi* (Enclosed Gardens). The architect was Andea Moroni. The

plants in the Garden itself may have been drawn from *The Carrara Herbal*, a fifteenth-century manuscript written for Francesco II, Lord of Padua (r.1390-1404), by the Augustinian, Jacopo Filippo. A translation from Arabic, the *Herbal* is derived from the work of the physician Serapion the Younger (c. 800).

29 *Hypnerotomachia*, p. 358.

30 *Ibid*, p. 362.

31 *Ibid*, p. 366.

Notes for Chapter 6

1 Frances Yates interprets the term pejoratively (*The Art of Memory*, p. 135). However see Copernicus, *De Revolutionibus*, trans. A.M. Duncan, (Barnes & Noble, 1976) p. 35, in which the term is meant simply to define the heavenly from the human. Translations of Copernicus's *De Revolutionibus* herein are from this edition.

2 *Liber de Sole*, in *Marsilii Ficini Florentini, …Opera* (Basel: Henric Petrina, [1576]), I, 966. English translation by Thomas Khun of Marsilio Ficino, *Liber de Sole*, reprinted by permission of the publisher from THE COPERNICAN REVOLUTION: PLANETARY ASTRONOMY IN THE DEVELOPMENT OF WESTERN THOUGHT, by Thomas S. Khun, p. 69, Cambridge, Mass.: Harvard University Press, Copyright © 1957 by the President and Fellows of Harvard College. Copyright © renewed, 1985 by Thomas S. Khun.

3 Bolzoni focuses on Camillo's literary achievements; Wenneker on his contribution to emblem literature; Yates assesses him in terms of the art of memory. Recently Hilary Gatti's work on the scientific work of Giordano Bruno has skipped over the influence of Camillo; see Gatti, Hilary, *Giordano Bruno and Renaissance Science*, (New York: Cornell University Press, 1999).

4 Nifo, Agostino, *In quattuor libros de cello et mundo et Aritote. et Avero. expositio*, bk. 2, fols. 23-6, quoted in Lattis, James M., *Between Copernicus and Galileo*, (Chicago: University of Chicago Press, 1994), p. 90.

5 According to North, 'Almost all of the astronomy known to the Christian scholar of the early Middle Ages came from one of seven authors…[namely] Pliny (first century A.D.), Martianus Capella (fifth century), and Isidore of Seville (seventh century) … a translation and commentary by Chalcidius (fourth century) of Plato's *Timaeus*… another commentary (fifth century) by Macrobius on a work called *Scipio's Dream*, by Cicero; … Boethius (sixth century); and … Bede (eighth century) North, J.D. *Stars, Minds and Fate, essays in Ancient and Medieval Cosmology* (London: Hambledon Press, 1989), p. 402. The influence of Arabic astronomy on that of the West was seminal, but is outwith the scope of this chapter to discuss. See also Robinson, K, 'The Celestial Streams of Giulio Camillo' *History of Science* 43 (2005), 321-41.

6 Cicero, *De Natura Deorum*, 37, quoted by Camillo in *L'Idea del Theatro*, p. 40.

7 The Baptistery itself dates from 1075. Menabuoi had completed most of the work on the interior by 1378. Previously, Menabuoi had worked for ten years with Giotto on the interior of the Scrovegni Chapel, and a clear relationship can be seen between the two in terms of shared pictorial conventions – Menabuoi's angels around the scene of the Crucifixion, for example, appear out of the sky around the head of Christ ringing their hands and weeping, or with their hands outstretched to the crowd of people below the Cross in a gesture of sorrow and surrender, in a way that is markedly similar to the angels that surround the mourners beside Giotto's body of Christ in the Scrovegni. Nevertheless, for all their pictorial similarities, the emphasis for each painter is different. Giotto's emotional force is, I think, matched by Menabuoi's metaphysics.

8 Prado, painted around 1505-10 The illustration shows the outer panel of the triptych which opens out to reveal the Garden within. Transparent, or semi-transparent, orbs of varying sizes form a recurrent visual motif in the inner painting. One prominent sphere, for example, in the middle panel, shows a man and woman inside, both of whom are faced with another glowing orange sphere that might be the inside of the flower, or it could be a sun.

9 Dante describes the movement in *Il Convivio* as being instigated by Intelligences, or angels ('substances separate from matter'). The tenth immovable sphere, according to Dante, 'announces the unity and stability of God.' This Empyrean Heaven is, he says, 'immovable, because it has within itself, in every part, that which its matter demands.' This is the reason that the *primum mobile* moves with such immense velocity: '…because [of] the fervent longing of all its parts to be united with those of this most quiet heaven…'. Dante, *The Banquet*, trans. Katherine Hillard, (London: Routledge & Kegan Paul, 1889), pp. 65-9.

10 The deferent was the imagined circular orbit of each of the planets and the sun around the earth.

11 Copernicus's teacher, Domenico da Novara, for example, ' held that no system so cumbersome and inaccurate as the Ptolemaic had become could possibly be true of nature', Kuhn, Thomas S., *The Copernican Revolution* (Harvard University Press, 1957), p. 69.

12 In his critique, Clavius complained that some of the homocentrists proposed up to seventy-nine spheres, for example. See Lattis, p. 94

13 Lattis, p. 90.

14 Donahue, William H. 'The Solid Planetary Spheres in Post-Copernican Natural Philosophy' in *The Copernican Achievement*, ed. Robert Westman (University of California Press: 1975), p. 273.

15 See Donahue, n.149.

16 Lattis, p. 94.

17 Jardine, Nicholas, 'The Significance of the Copernican Orbs' *Journal for the History of Astronomy* 12 (1981), p. 171.

18 Pontano, Giovanni Giovano, *Opera*, (Venice, 1512).

19 Abano, Pietro d', *Tractatus de venenis* (Mantua: T. Septemcastrensem & Johannes Burster, 1473).

20 Camillo, *L'Idea del Theatro*, p. 14.

21 Clavius, *Sphaera* (1611), p. 48, quoted in Lattis, p. 104.

22 Giannettasio, Nicola Partenio *Universalis cosmographiae elementata* (1688), quoted in Lattis, p. 103.

23 Camillo, *L'Idea del Theatro, p. 29.*

24 The idea of the waters above the heavens is derived from Genesis 1:7.

25 Camillo, *L'Idea del Theatro, p. 22.*

26 *Ibid.*, p 23.

27 *Ibid.*, p. 30.

28 *Ibid.*, p. 38.

29 The idea of a mystical 'dew' was common parlance in alchemical treatises, and it is appropriate here to mention the probable influence on Camillo of Paracelsus (or Theophrastus Bombastus von Hohenheim (1493-1541)), whose alchemical works were widespread.

30 Camillo, *L'Idea del Theatro*, p. 41.

31 *Ibid.*, p. 38.

32 In the King James version, the translation of the relevant verse loses the reference to 'channels'. Song of Solomon 7:5 *Thine head upon thee is like Carmel, and the hair of thine head like purple; the king is held in the galleries*

33 King James Version Psalm 133: *Behold, how good and how pleasant it is for brethren to dwell together in unity!*

It is like the precious ointment upon the head, that ran down upon the beard, even Aaron's beard: that went down to the skirts of his garments;

As the dew of Hermon, and as the dew that descended upon the mountains of Zion: for there the Lord commanded the blessing, even life for evermore.

34 *Luke 12:7, quoted in L'Idea del Theatro, p. 24.*

35 There are four sources of paper in *De Revolutionibus*, from papermills throughout Europe. The oldest has a Hippocampus watermark. See, 'Nicholas Copernicus Complete Works I', *The Manuscript of Nicholas Copernicus' 'On the Revolutions' Facsimile* (Warsaw: Macmillan & Polish Scientific Publishers, 1972).

36 I cannot find precise dates for the period when Camillo studied at Padua, but it is reasonable to estimate that it would have been in the years around 1500. We can date Copernicus's time at Padua from 1501 –1503. (He took his doctorate at Ferrara in 1503). Copernicus was a student at Bologna from 1497 to around 1500. Camillo is believed to have held a Chair of Dialectics at Bologna from around 1521-25.

37 Jardine, 'The Significance of the Copernican Orbs', p. 176.

38 See Westman, Robert, 'Proof, poetics and patronage' in *Reappraisals of the Scientific Revolution*, ed. David C. Lindberg & Robert S. Westman (University of Cambridge Press, 1990) p. 168, for discussion of Duhem's, Burtt's and Kuhn's approach.

39 Jardine, 'The Significance of the Copernican Orbs', p. 168.

40 See Westman, pp. 179-182.

41 Paolo Rossi, Hermeticism and Rationality' in *Reason, Experiment and Mysticism in the Scientific Revolutuon*, eds. M.L. Righini Bonelli William R. Shea, (London: Macmillan Press, 1975), p. 259.

42 Westman, 'Proof, poetics and Patronage: Copernicus's preface to *De Revolutionibus*' p. 167-205.

43 Yates, Frances, *Giordano Bruno and the Hermetic Tradition*, (London: Routledge & Kegan Paul, 1964), p. 153.

44 Camillo begins *L'Idea del Theatro* by saying: 'The oldest and wisest writers always have had the habit of protecting in their writings the secrets of God with dark veils, so that they are understood only by those, who (as Christ says) 'have ears to hear', that is, those who are chosen by God to understand His most holy mysteries.' p. 7.

45 Most of the astronomical observations of the book, however, were made at Frauenberg, where Copernicus settled in 1512.

46 Later, in 1514, he was invited to return to Italy by Bernhard Sculteti, Chaplain to the Pope to take part in the deliberations on calendar reform, though Copernicus refused the invitation on the grounds that calendar reform was impossible until the problem of the motions of the Sun and Moon had been resolved. He was not only known as an astronomer, however. When in Poland, as a Canon at Frauenberg, he had other duties which required of him further skills. In 1522, for example, he presented a treatise on economic reform to the Prussian Diet advocating monetary union between neighbouring states.

47 The beginning of Osiander's *To the Reader on the Hypotheses in this Work* reads: 'I have no doubt that certain learned men, now that the novelty of the hypotheses in this work has been widely reported – for it establishes that the Earth moves, and indeed that the sun is motionless in the middle of the universe – are extremely shocked, and think that the scholarly disciplines, rightly established once and for all, should not be upset...' Copernicus, *De Revolutionibus*, p. 22.

48 *Ibid*, p. 23.

49 *Ibid.*, p. 24.

50 Camillo, *L'Idea del Theatro*, p. 7.

51 Copernicus, *De Revolutionibus*, Book One, Ch. X1.

52 Camillo ascribes the simile of giving birth to the earth in *L'Idea del Theatro*, p. 38, and to the heat from the sun at p. 20 equating the movement of birth to both.

53 *Ibid*, p. 20.

[54] *Ibid.*, p. 38.
[55] *De Revolutionibus*, p. 50.
[56] *L'idea del Theatro*, p. 14.
[57] *Ibid.*, p. 26.
[58] *Ibid.*, p. 15.
[59] *Ibid.*, p. 71. There are three appearances of the fates image, all of them in this central column of the Theatre. The interpretations he gives for each of the images are as follows: '…the Fates, symbols of destiny, of the cause, of the beginning, of the event, of the effect and of the end.' (p. 16). 'The fates: to give cause, to begin, to lead to the end.' (p. 77).

Notes for Chapter 7

[1] *The Theatre of Memory*, VRML model, 2001. Made in collaboration with Carl Smith.

[2] *Utriusque Cosmi*, itself, is a strange compendium that bridges subjects from creation, to musical instruments, to the inner workings of the eye, to strategies for battle.

[3] Filippo Brunelleschi is credited with being the first to systematize a theory of perspective, in the creation of the Duomo in Florence, completed in 1436. Subsequently, Leon Battista Alberti developed this in terms of painting, with the publication of his *Della Pittura* (1436), and in architecture, with *De Re Ædificatoria* (1485).

[4] Serlio, Sebastiano, trans., Allardyce Nicoll, *The Second Book of Architecture (Il Primo (Secondo) Libro d'Architettura)*, Paris, 1545, in Hewitt, Barnard ed., *The Renaissance Stage, Documents of Serlio, Sabbattini, and Furttenbach* (University of Miami Press, 1958), pp. 63-74.

[5] Koyré, Alexander, *From the Closed World to the Infinite Universe*, (Baltimore: Johns Hopkins Press, 1957), p. 6.

[6] That is, 'not only that [the universe] is boundless and is not terminated by an outside shell, but also that it is not "terminated" in its constituents…that it utterly lacks precision and strict determination'. See Koyré, p. 8.

[7] Macneice, Louis, *Snow*, January, 1935.

[8] Cusa, Nicolaus, *De docta ignorantia*, 1. II, cap. ii, p. 102, quoted in Koyré, p. 17.

[9] Koyré, pp. 9-12.

Note for Epigraph

[1] Achille Bocchi's *Symbolicae quaestiones* (Bologna: Nuova Accademia Bocciana, 1555). Contentio Lusciniae ob Victoriam. Iulio Camillo Foroiuliensi Symb. LXXXVI (Bk 3, p. CLXXXI).

'Five books of questions in symbol forms concerning universal creation, the subject of serious play.'

Bibliography

Adams, Alison, Rawles, Stephen & Saunders, Alison, *A Bibliography of French Emblem Books* (Geneva: Droz, 1999-2002).

Allen, Michael J.B., *The Platonism of Marsilio Ficino* (Berkeley: University of California Press, 1984).

Baring, Anne & Cashford, Jules, *The Myth of the Goddess: Evolution of an Image* (London: Penguin, 1993).

Barker, William, *The Adages of Erasmus* (Toronto: University of Toronto Press, 2001).

Bolgar, R.R., *The Classical Heritage and its Beneficiaries* (Cambridge: Cambridge University Press, 1954).

Bolzoni, Lina, trans. Jeremy Parzen, *The Gallery of Memory: Literary and Iconographic Models in the Age of the Printing Press* (Toronto: University of Toronto Press, 2001).

_____ 'Giulio Camillo and Emblems' (Unpublished paper), from Sixth International Emblem Conference, La Coruña, Spain.

_____ *Il teatro della memoria: studi su G. Camillo* (Padua: Liviana, 1984).

_____ 'Erasmo e Camillo: il dibattito sul'imitazione', *Filologia antica e moderna*, 4 (1993), 69-113.

Bonelli, M.L. Righini & Shea,William R. (eds), *Reason ,Experiment and Mysticism in the Scientific Revolutuon* (London: Macmillan Press, 1975).

Boyle, Marjorie O'Rourke, *Christening Pagan Mysteries; Erasmus in Pursuit of Wisdom* (Toronto: University of Toronto Press, 1981).

_____ *Erasmus on Language and Method in Theology* (Toronto: University of Toronto Press, 1977).

Buller, John. *Proenca/Theatre of Memory*. Sarah Walker. BBC Symphony Orchestra. Cond. Mark Elder. 2003. B00009W8NZ.

Bury, M., *The Print in Italy 1550-1620* (London: British Museum Press, 2001).

Buzan, Tony, *Use Your Memory* (London: BBC Books, 1996).

Callahan, Virginia W., 'The Erasmus-Hercules Equation in the Emblems of Alciati' published in Selig, Karl-Ludwig and Sears, Elizabeth, *The Verbal and The Visual: Essays in honor of William Sebastian Heckscher* (New York: Italica Press, 1990).

Camillo Delminio, Giulio, ed. Lina Bolzoni, *L'Idea del Theatro e altri scritti di retorica* (Turin: Edizioni RES, 1990).

_____ trans. Francoise Graziani, with introduction and notes by Lina Bolzoni, *De L'Imitation* (Paris: Les Belles Lettres, 1996).

Carruthers, Mary, *The Book of Memory* (Cambridge: Cambridge University Press, 1990).

_____ *The Craft of Thought* (Cambridge University Press, 1998).

Caulfield, Carlota, trans. Mary G. Berg, *The Book of Giulio Camillo* (InteliBooks Publishers, 2003).

Cellini, Benvenuto, trans. John Addington Symonds, *Auto-*

biography of Benvenuto Cellini (New York: Anchor Books, 1975).

Cicero, trans. F.B. Calvert, *De Oratore* (Edinburgh: Edmonston & Douglas, 1870).

____ trans. J.G.F. Powell, *Laelius, On Friendship & The Dream of Scipio* (England: Aris & Phillips, 1990).

Cirillo, Madeleine, B. 'Giulio Bonasone and Sixteenth-Century Printmaking' (unpublished PhD Thesis: University of Wisconsin, 1978).

Chomarat, Jacques, *Grammaire et Rhetorique Chez Erasme*, vols 1 & 2 (Paris: Les Belles Lettres, 1981).

Colonna, Francesco, translation and notes Joscelyn Godwin, *Hypnerotomachia Poliphili* (London: Thames & Hudson, 1999).

Copenhaver, Brian P., *Hermetica*, (Cambridge: Cambridge University Press, 1992).

Copernicus, Nicholas, trans. A.M. Duncan, *On the Revolution of the Heavenly Spheres* (Barnes & Noble, 1976).

____ 'On the Revolutions' Facsimile* (Warsaw: Macmillan and Polish Scientific Publishers,1972).

Daly, Peter, M. & Manning, John, *Aspects of Renaissance and Baroque Symbol Theory 1500-1700* (New York: AMS Press, 1999).

Damasio, Antonio, *The Feeling of What Happens* (London: Vintage, 2000).

Dante, trans. Katherine Hillard, *The Banquet* (London: Routledge & Kegan Paul, 1889).

____ trans. Mark Musa, *The Divine Comedy, vol. III: Paradise* (London: Penguin Books, 1984).

De Luca, Elena, 'Silent Meanings: Emblems, Lay Culture and Political Awareness in Sixteenth-Century Bologna', *Emblematica*, 12 (2002) 61-81.

DeMolen, Richard L. (ed.), *Essays on the Works of Erasmus* (USA: Yale University Press, 1978).

Dickens, A.G. & Whitney, R.D. Jones, *Erasmus the Reformer* (London: Methuen, 1994).

Dubuffet, Jean, *Theatre De Memoire*, unlimited edition print, 1977.

Eco, Umberto, Review of Mario Turello, Daniele Cortolezzis: Anima Artificiale. Il Teatro magico di Giulio Camillo, in *L'Espresso*, 14 August 1988.

Edwards, John, *The Jews in Christian Europe 1400-1700* (London: Routledge, 1988).

Eliade, Mircea, trans. Willard R. Trask, *The Myth of The Eternal Return* (London: Arkana, 1989).

Engel, William, *Mapping Mortality* (University of Massachusetts Press, 1995).

Erasmus, ed. A.H.T. Levi, *Collected Works of Erasmus 28: Ciceronianus*, (Toronto: University of Toronto Press, 1986).

____ ed. Craig R. Thompson, *Collected Works of Erasmus Vol. 23: Antibarbari/Parabolae* (Toronto: University of Toronto Press, 1978).

____ trans. R.A.B. Mynors & Alexander Dalzell, *The Correspondence of Erasmus, 1523-1524*, (Toronto: University of Toronto Press, 1992)

____ ed. H.M. Allen, *Opus Epistolarum Des. Erasmi Roterdami* (Oxford: Oxford University Press, 1937).

Farge, J.K., *Orthodoxy and Reform in Early Reformation France* (Leiden: E.J. Brill, 1985).

Fahy, Conor, review of Hobson, Anthony, *Renaissance Book Collecting: Jean Grolier and Diego Hurtado de Mendoza, Their Books and Bindings* (Cambridge University Press, 1999) in *Italian Studies*, LVI, 2001.

Ficino, M., trans. Michael J.B. Allen, *The Philebus Commentary* (Berkeley: University of California Press, 1975).

____ *Omnia Opere Plotini*, ed. Frederick Creuzer (Oxford: Oxford University Press, 1835).

Finaldi, Gabriele, with intro. by Neil MacGregor, *The Image of Christ*, the catalogue of the exhibition *Seeing Salvation*, (London: National Gallery Co., distributed by Yale University Press, 2000).

Fracastorii, Heironymi, *De Contagione et Contagiosis Morbis et eorum Curatione, Libri III*, translation and notes Wilmer Cave Wright (New York: Putnam, 1930).

Gaeta, Franco, *Un Nuncio Pontificio A Venezia nel Cinquecento (Girolamo Aleandro)* (Venice: Instituto per la Collaborazione Cultural, 1960).

Gatti, Hilary, *Giordano Bruno & Renaissance Science* (USA: Cornell University Press, 2002).

Gingerich, Owen *The Great Copernicus Chase and Other Adventures in Astronomical History* (Sky Publishing Corp. & Cambridge University Press, 1992).

Green-Pederson, Niels Jørgen, *The Tradition of the Topics in the Middle Ages* (Munich: Philosophia Verlag, 1984).

Greenfield, Susan, *Brain Story* (London: BBC Worldwide, 2000).

Hale, J.R., *Renaissance Europe 1480-1520* (London: Fontana, 1971).

Halkin, Léon-E., *Erasmus* (Oxford: Blackwell, 1994).

Hartnoll, Phyllis, *The Theatre: a concise history* (London: Thames & Hudson, 1985).

Hewitt, Barnard (ed.), *The Renaissance Stage: Documents of Serlio, Sabbattini, and Furttenbach* (USA: University of Miami Press, 1958).

Hughes, Ted, *Shakespeare and the Goddess of Complete Being* (London: Faber & Faber, 1992).

Jardine, Nicholas, 'The Significance of the Copernican Orbs' *Journal for the History of Astronomy*, 13 (1982), 168-94.

____ & Cunningham, Andrew, (eds). *Romanticism and the Sciences* (Cambridge: Cambridge University Press, 1990).

Jasper, David & Prickett, Stephen (eds.), *The Bible and Literature: a reader* (Oxford: Blackwell Publishers, 1999).

Jung, Carl, trans., R.F.C. Hull, *Psychology and Alchemy* (London: Routledge & Kegan Paul, 1980).

Kemp, Martin & Wallace, Marina, *Spectacular Bodies* (London: Hayward Gallery Publishing, 2000).

Klestinec, C., 'History of Anatomy Theaters in Sixteenth-Century Padua' *Journal of the History of Medicine and Allied Sciences*, 59 (3) (2004), 375-412.

Koyré, Alexander, *From the Closed World to the Infinite Universe* (Baltimore: Johns Hopkins Press, 1957).

Kuhn, Thomas S., *The Copernican Revolution* (Cambridge: Harvard University Press, 1957).

Lattis, James M., *Between Copernicus and Galileo* (Chicago: University of Chicago Press, 1994),

Levere, T.H. & Shea, W.R. (eds.), *Nature, Experiment and the Sciences* (Dordrecht: Kluwer Academic Publishers, 1990).

Levi, Anthony, *Renaissance and Reformation* (USA: Yale University Press, 2002).

Lindberg, David C. & Westman, Robert S. (eds.), *Reappraisals of the Scientific Revolution* (Cambridge: Cambridge University Press, 1990).

Loach, Judi 'Architecture and Emblematics', in *Emblems and Art History* vol 1 (Glasgow: Glasgow Emblem Studies, 1996) 1-21.

MacGregor, Neil, with Erika Langmuir, *Seeing Salvation* (London: BBC Worldwide., 2000).

Markowitz, Karen & Jensen, Eric, *The Great Memory Book* (Brain Store, 1999).

Massari, Stefania, *Giulio Bonasone*, vols. 1 & 2 (Rome: Edizioni Quasar, 1983)

Mattusek, Peter, précis of web-sites/art projects devoted to 'Memory Theatres': www.sfb-performativ.de

McConica, James, *Erasmus* (Oxford: Oxford University Press,1991).

Mandou, Robert, *From Humanism to Science 1480-1700* (London: Penguin, 1978).

Nolte, John, *The Human Brain: an Introduction to its Functional Anatomy*, (Missouri: Mosby, 1999).

North, J.D. *Stars, Minds and Fate: Essays in Ancient and Medieval Cosmology* (London: The Hambledon Press, 1989).

Norton, David, *A History of the Bible as Literature* (Cambridge: Cambridge University Press, 1993).

O' Brien, Dominic, *The Amazing Memory Book* (London: Duncan Baird Publishers, 2001).

Oestrich, Gerhard, trans. David McLintock, *Neostoicism and the Early Modern State* (Cambridge: Cambridge University Press, 1982).

Oeuvres Poétiques: François 1er, ed. J.E. Kane (Geneva: Slatkine, 1984).

Panofsky, Erwin, *Meaning in the Visual Arts* (London: Penguin, 1993).

Pigman III, G.W. 'Imitation and the Renaissance Sense of the past: the reception of Erasmus' *Ciceronianus*,' *Journal for Medieval and Renaissance Studies*, 9 (1979) 155-77.

Ramachandran, V.S. & Blakeslee, Sandra, *Phantoms in the Brain* (London: Fourth Estate, 1988).

Rice Jr, Eugene F., 'Humanist Aristotelianism in France: Jacques Lefèvre d'Étaples and his circle' in *Humanism in France*, ed. A.H.T. Levi (Manchester: Manchester University Press, 1970),

Robinson, K, 'A Search for the Source of the Whirlpool of Artifice', (Glasgow University, PhD thesis, 2002).

___'Power and Persuasion in the Theatre of Camillo', ed. Urszula Szulakowska, *Power and Persuasion: Sculpture in its Rhetorical Context* (Warsaw: Institute of Art of the Polish Academy of Sciences, 2004) 37-48.

___'Fame with Tongue', *Reformation and Renaissance Review*, 6 (2004) 107-123.

___'The Celestial Streams of Giulio Camillo', *History of Science*, 43 (2005) 321-41.

Roob, Alexander, *Alchemy and Mysticism* (Taschen, 1997).

Roth, Cecil, *The History of the Jews in Venice* (New York: Schocken Books, 1975).

Russell, Daniel, *Emblematic Structures in Renaissance French Culture* (Toronto: University of Toronto Press, 1995).

Sandys, J.E., *Harvard Lectures on the Revival of Learning* (Cambridge: Cambridge University Press, 1905).

Scaliger, Jules-Cesar, Ed. Michel Magnien, *Orationes Duae Contra Erasmum, Oratio Pro. M. Tullio Cicerone Contra Des. Erasmum* (1531) & *Adversus Des. Erasmi Roterod. Dialogum Ciceronianum Oratio Secunda* (1537) (Geneva: Droz, 1999).

Schama, Simon, *Landscape and Memory* (London: Fontana Press, 1995).

Schmitt, Charles B. *Aristotle and the Renaissance* (London: Harvard University Press, 1983).

___ *Renaissance Averroism studied through the Venetian Editions of Aristotle-Averroës* (Rome: Accademia Nazionale dei Luicei, 1979).

___ *The Aristotelian Tradition & Renaissance Universities* (Aldershot: Variorum, 1984).

___ *The Cambridge History of Renaissance Philosophy* (Cambridge: Cambridge University Press, 1988).

Seigel, Jerrold E., *Rhetoric and Philosophy in Renaissance Humanism: the union of eloquence and wisdom, Petrarch to Valla* (Princeton: Princeton University Press, 1968).

Singer, Charles *A Short History of Scientific Ideas* (Oxford: Oxford University Press, 1959).

Stegmann, André, 'Erasme et la France (1495-1520)' in *Colloquium Erasmianum: Actes du Colloque International réuni à Mons...*(Mons: 1968).

Szönyi, György E., 'Architectural Symbolism and Fantasy Land-scapes in Alchemical and Occult Discourse: Revelatory Images' in *Emblems & Alchemy*, vol. 3, ed. Alison Adams & Stanton J. Linden (Glasgow: Glasgow Emblem Studies, 1998) 49-69.

Valla, Lorenzo *De Voluptate*, trans. A. Kent Hieatt & Maristella

Lorch, with Intro by Lorch (New York: Arabis, 1977).

Viola, Bill, *Reasons for Knocking at an Empty House*, (Cambridge MA: MIT Press in association with Anthony d'Offay Gallery, London, 1995).

___ *Theatre of Memory*. Video installation. Newport Harbor Art Museum. 1985.

Walker, Barbara G., *The Woman's Encyclopedia of Myths and Secrets* (San Francisco: Harper & Row, 1983).

Warner, Marina, *Monuments and Maidens* (London: Weidenfeld & Nicolson, 1985).

Watson, Elisabeth See, *Achille Bocchi and the Emblem Book as Symbolic Form* (Cambridge: Cambridge University Press, 1993).

Wenneker, Lu Beery, 'An Examination of L'Idea del Theatro of Giulio Camillo, including an annotated translation, with special attention to his influence on Emblem Literature and Iconography', (unpublished PhD Thesis: University of Pittsburgh, 1970).

Westman, Robert S. (ed.), *The Copernican Achievement* (Berkeley: University of California Press, 1975).

Whitfield, Peter, *The Mapping of the Heavens* (London: British Library, 1995).

Wilson, Robert, *Astronomy through the Ages* (London: Taylor & Francis, 1997).

Wylie, James A., *The History of Protestantism*, vol. II, Bk XIII, Ch. XVIII (London: Cassell, 1878), quoted at www.doctrine.org/history.

Yates, Frances A., *Ideas and Ideals in the North European Renaissance, Collected Essays*, vol. 3, (London: Routledge & Kegan Paul, 1984).

___ *Giordano Bruno and the Hermetic Tradition* (London: Routledge & Kegan Paul, 1964).

___ *The Occult Philosophy in the Elizabethan Age* (London: Ark, 1983).

___ *The Art of Memory* (London: Pimlico, 1992).

Bibliography: Sources

Abano, Pietro d', *Conciliator differentiarum philosophorum et precipue medicorum Petri de Abano* (Mantua: Thomas Septemcastrensem & Johannes Burster de Capidona, 1472).

___ *Conciliator Differentiarum Philosophorum: Et Praecipue Medicorum Petri De Abano. Tractatus De Veneni* (Venice: Gabriele de Tarvisio, 1476).

___ *Tractatus de venenis* (Mantua: T. Septemcastrensem & Johannes Burster, 1473).

Alciato, Andrea, *Emblematum Libellus, Nuper in Lucem Editus* (Venice: Aldus Manutius, 1546).

Altani, Federigo. Count, 'Memorie intorno alla vita ed all' opere di G. Camillo Delminio' in *Nuova Raccolta d'opuscoli scientifici e Filologici*, vol. 1. (Venice: Simone Occhi, 1755).

Apian, Petrus, *Cosmographia* (Antwerp, 1584).

Bocchi, Achille, *Symbolicarum quaestionum de universo genere quas serio ludebat libri quinque* ... (Bologna: In aedib. Novae Academiae Boccianae, 1555).

Camillo Delminio, Giulio, *L'Idea del Theatro* (Florence: Lorenzo Torentino, 1550).

___ *Due Trattati ... l'uno delle Materie, che possono uenir sotto lo stile dell'eloquente: l'altro dell' Imitazione* (Venice: Farri, 1544).

___ *L'Opere di M. Giulio Camillo* (Venice: Farri, 1579).

___ *Tutte le opere* [Preface by Lodovico Dolce.] (Venice: G. Giolito de Ferrari, & Fratelli, 1552).

Citolini, Allesandro, *La Tipocosmia* (Venice: V. Valgrisi, 1561).

Colonna, Francesco, *Hypnerotomachia Poliphili* (Venice: Aldus Manutius, 1499).

Copernicus, Nicolaus, *De revolutionibus orbium coelestium* (Nuremberg, 1543).

Dolce, Ludovico, *Dialogo della Pittura* (Venice: Appresso Gabries Giolito De'Ferrari, 1557).

Fludd, Robert, *Utriusque cosmic maioris scilicet et minoris metaphysica, physica atque technical historia…Tomi I. II.*, (Oppenheim: 1617).

Johnson, Thomas, *Cornucopiae, or Diverse Secrets: Wherein is contained the rare secrets in Man, Beasts, Foules, Fishes, Trees, Plantes, stones and such like* (London: William Barley, 1596).

Kircher, Athanasius, *Ars magna lucis* (Amsterdam: [n.p.], 1671).

Lomazzo, Giovanni Paolo, *Idea del tempio della pittura di Gio. Paolo Lomazzo ... Nella quale egli discorre dell' origine, & fondamento delle cose contenute nel suo Trattato dell' arte della pittura ...* (Milan: Per Paolo Gottardo Pontio, 1590).

___ *A Tracte Containing the Artes of curious Painting, Carving & Building*, trans: Richard Haydocke (Oxford: Joseph Barnes, 1598).

Perriere, Guillaume de la, *Le Theatre de bons engines* (Lyons: Denis de Harsy 1540).

Petrarch, Francesco, *Il Petrarcha* [with G. Camillo's MS. Notes in G. Amelonghi's autograph.] (Venice: Aldus Manutius, 1514).

Pontano, Giovanni Giovano, *De Rebus Coelestibus Libri X1111* (Florence, 1520).

___ *Opera* (Venice, 1512).

Sacro Bosco, Joannes de, *Libellus de sphaera cum praefacione Philippi Melanthonis* (Antwerp: Ioannes Richard, 1543).

___ *Spera mundi* (Venice: Franciscus Renner, de Heilbronn, 1478).

Van Veen, Otto, *Historia septem infantium de Lara ...* (Antwerp: Philippum Lisaert, 1612).

Valeriano, G. P. & Curione, C. A., *Hieroglyphica* (Basel: Per Thomam Guarinum, 1567).

Image Credits

All reasonable efforts have been taken to obtain permission to reproduce material from sources. In the event of a query, please contact the publishers.

Image from *The Theatre of Memory*, VRML model, Kate Robinson and Carl Smith, 2001. Further images of this model are on pp. 125, 128 and 129.

Uroboros from Horapollo's *Hieroglyphica*, (Bologna, 1517). Reprinted by kind permission of the University of Glasgow Library Special Collections Department.

Images on pp. 28, 30, 31, 32, 33, 34, 64, 65, 80, 87, 88, 93, 115 and 123 from *The Theatre of Memory*, Kate Robinson, 2001.

Whirlpool Galaxy. January 2005. NASA, ESA, S. Beckwith (STScI), and The Hubble Heritage Team (STScI/AURA).

Illuminated letters on pp. 5, 21, 41, 55, 79, 103 and 126 from *De Revolutionibus Orbium Coelestium* by Nicolaus Copernicus, (Nuremberg, 1543). Reprinted by kind permission of the University of Glasgow Library Special Collections Department.

p.6 *Lion sculpture* by A. Cain, 1866. Bronze, 2 x 1 x 1.5 m. Photograph by KR.

p.8 *Sprouting Tree*, Botanic Gardens, Glasgow, 2002.

p.10 Map from *The Art of Memory* by Frances Yates, published by Pimlico. Reprinted by permission of The Random House Group Ltd.

p.11 *Juno on a Swing*, by KR. Acrylic on canvas. 43 x 52 cm. 2001. Photograph by M. Muirhead, 2005.

p.12 *Hippocampus*, by KR. Ink on paper. 69 x 139 cm. 2001. Photograph by M. Muirhead, 2005.

p.13 *Heart*, by KR. Bronze, mirror and stained glass. 26 x 31 x 31cm. 2001. Photograph by M. Muirhead, 2005.

p.19 *Artificiosa rota*, by Giulio Camillo. *Opere di M. Giulio Camillo, etc.* (Venice: Farri, 1579). Reprinted by permission of The Trustees of the National Library of Scotland.

p.35 *Rhetorical tree diagram*, by Giulio Camillo. *Opere di M. Giulio Camillo, etc.* (Venice: Farri, 1579). Reprinted by permission of The Trustees of the National Library of Scotland.

p.36 In homage to *Branching, Matrix and Schizo Structures* by Bill Viola. *Reasons for Knocking at an Empty House*, (MIT Press in association with the Anthony D'Offay Gallery, London, 1995).

p.37 Map courtesy Lumeta Corp. Map Copyright © Lumeta 2005.

Line drawings on pp. 54, 56, 60, 66, 68, 69, 87, 89, 90 and 94 from *Hypnerotomachia Poliphili: The Strife of Love in a Dream* by Francesco Colonna, translated by Joscelyn Godwin. © Joscelyn Godwin 1999. Reprinted by kind permission of Thames & Hudson Ltd., London.

pp.74-5 *Arma Christi*. German, Lower Rhine or Westphalia. Elephant ivory with painted and gilded leaves. 10.5 x 5.9 cm. V & A Images/Victoria and Albert Museum.

pp.84-5 *Plan of Venice*, by Odoardo Fialetti, 16th-17th century, NO DATA Provost and Fellows of Eton College, Windsor, UK.; Bridgeman Art Library.

p.97 *Model of the Anatomy Theatre*. University of Padua.

p.99 *Map of the Botanical Garden at Padua.*

p.104 *Geographia*, by Ptolemy (Strasbourg, 1513). Reprinted by kind permission of the University of Glasgow Library Special Collections Department.

p.106 *La Creazione del Mondo*, by Giusto de'Menabuoi. Approx. 12 x 6m. Baptistery of Padua Cathedral.

p.108 *The Creation of the World*, closed doors of the triptych *The Garden of Earthly Delights*, c.1500 by Hieronymous Bosch (c.1450-1516). Oil on panel, 220 x 195 cm. Museo del Prado, Madrid. Bridgeman Art Library.

p.109 *Diagram*, by Peter Apian. *Cosmographia* (Antwerp, 1584). Reprinted by kind permission of the University of Glasgow Library Special Collections Department.

p.121 *Diagram, De Revolutionibus Orbium Coelestium* by Nicolaus Copernicus, (Nuremberg, 1543). Reprinted by kind permission of the University of Glasgow Library Special Collections Department.

pp.126-7 *Et sic in infinitum* by Robert Fludd. *Utriusque Cosmi maioris scilicet et minoris metaphysica* (Oppenheim, 1617). Reprinted by kind permission of the University of Glasgow Library Special Collections Department.

pp.132-3 *Plan of Theatre* by Sebastiano Serlio. *Il primo [secondo] libro d'architettura di Sebastiano* (Venice: Per Gio. Battista, & Marchion Sessa fratelli, 1560.) Reprinted by kind permission of University of Glasgow Library Special Collections Department.

p.135 *Artificiosa rota*, by Giulio Camillo. *Due trattati: l'uno delle materie, che possono uenir sotto lo stile dell'eloquente: l'altro della imitatione.* (Venice: Farri, 1544). Reprinted by permission of The Trustees of the National Library of Scotland.

p.138 *Emblem for Giulio Camillo*, probably by Giulio Bonasone. From *Symbolicarum quaestionum de universo genere quas serio ludebat libri quinque ...* by Achille Bocchi. (Bologna: Novae Academiae Bocchianae, 1555). Reprinted by kind permission of the University of Glasgow Library Special Collections Department.

Index

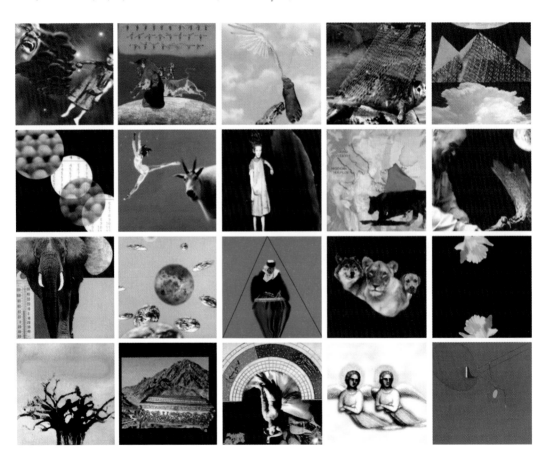